This Is Heaven?
A tale set in the realm beyond the door we call DEATH

By

J.G. Rockell

Presented by
Janet Bates

Copyright © 2023 by – Janet Bates – All Rights Reserved.

It is not legal to reproduce, duplicate, or transmit any part of this document in either electronic means or printed format. Recording of this publication is strictly prohibited.

Table of Contents

Dedication	i
Acknowledgement	ii
About the Author	iii
Foreword	iv
The Transition	1
Rebellion	9
Runaway	23
Capture	29
Moira's Experience	40
Paul's New Friends	50
Moira's Education Begins	63
Paul's Journey	74
Moira Settling In	83
Paul and Jane	91
Moira at School	118
Paul Meets Sean	131
The Search	174
Cross Communication	200
Walkabout	215
Re-union	236
An Old Friend	245

Dedication

I believe Jack would dedicate this book to readers and enquiring minds around the world. With love, he would also dedicate it to his wife of 50 years, Joan, and his son Clive (both deceased) and daughter Janet, and her two children, Carolyn and Tim (now adults, whom he loved dearly). I, as his daughter, would like to dedicate it to Jack himself. He inspired and supported me in every way ~ JB

Acknowledgements

I must single out my cousin Julia, who brought to my attention the poor health and short lifespan of Jack's manuscript, as it had deteriorated greatly from when I last looked at it. This shocked me into action. Re-reading it now after about 30 years, I was touched, and proud of his work. I can hear his voice clearly, and he wrote it as he spoke. His sense of humour, knowledge and desire to share, rings true in the text. I am so proud of him.

Lastly, I must acknowledge my husband Ned. He and Jack were kindred spirits, both very spiritual and gifted healers. More importantly, however, this book would not have been rejuvenated without the wholehearted support and encouragement of Ned, Thank you.

About the Author

J.G. Rockell 1921-2000 lived his entire life in New Zealand, except when fighting in WWII. He wrote this book around 1988, to share the learnings fed to him from the "other side." To save this manuscript from deterioration and to complete his unfinished business, we decided to publish his work in 2023, as the manuscript was almost indecipherable by this time.

Foreword

Dear Reader, Allow me to introduce myself. My name is Janet Bates, and I am the only daughter of Jack Rockell. I did have a brother also, but he passed away in 2022. Working on this book, retyping it out, sometimes with the aid of a magnifying glass, laughing and crying both, as Jack was on my left shoulder directing the work. It has been a privilege, honour and challenge. I know Dad/Jack is happy for this to be printed and distributed widely.

The author of this book was my late father, John (known as Jack) Rockell. He was born in New Zealand, in 1921, and passed away in the year 2000, a month or two short of his 80th birthday. He was a very interesting and interested man. He was interested in everything and everybody. He was a student of life; despite having to leave school at 14, he continued to study life, people, electronics (radios and television), he loved music, sailing and flying, and family. He mastered so many "hobbies". His all-consuming passion was figuring out how everything worked and fitted into the grand scheme of things. He was a talented healer and clairvoyant later in his life. This book was his way to share his knowledge of the teachings, as he describes "meticulously fed to us from the upper realms" in an understandable non-technical way. He typed up his manuscript before 1988; no word processors or spell check available then. The manuscript has been stored, but over the past 20 years, it has deteriorated almost beyond being able to read it in places. Thanks to a dear cousin wanting to relook at "Dad's book," I was alerted to the poor state it was in. She carefully transcribed several pages, prompting me to "redo" the whole thing – for posterity's sake. Thank you, Julia.

Very little has been changed, as I wanted it to be in his voice, which was feeding me tips as I worked, and although I had read this years ago, it was still an emotional experience hearing his words and remembering discussions we'd had on these topics in my teens (1960's). Have a read and accept what resonates with you – you will find your own truths.

I am grateful he left me with this legacy and honoured to preserve its existence. He was a treasured and loved Husband, Father, Grandfather, Friend, Teacher, and Uncle when it was his time to leave us and rest. He is still very much missed and loved – and I suspect he didn't rest long on arrival "over there."

I love you, Dad, but you know that. xx

Janet Bates (nee Rockell)

The Transition

Paul Askew laughed as he hauled the car, tyres screaming, around the tight bend in the narrow hill road, determined to keep the car in front close enough to nip past at the first opportunity. The tail lights ahead winked out at the bend ahead. "I'll get him! You watch; I'll get him on the next straight bit!" as he cleared the bend, the tail lights ahead still disappeared around the bend, so he put his foot down, unmindful of the fact they were going down a steep hill.

"Paul! Paul!" the girl beside him screamed. "Go easy for God's sake! You're going 'way too fast……"

"Na! I can handle this – you watch me catch them!" Swinging wildly, they entered the next bend.

"Please!" "You'll kill us both! Forget the stupid race!" Paul laughed again. "Look! I'm gaining on them! Catch them, next straight bit. I will!"

"I wouldn't have come with you if I'd seen you were so drunk," the girl cried. "You're mad driving like this!"

But Paul was not listening. "Look, Moira. I know what I'm doing! See! I've closed the gap!"

They had been at a rave-up over at Silverstream and were on their way back to Featherston, racing with the car in front, carrying the two friends who had challenged him. Over the Rimutaka Range, difficult enough at any time, but when you're full of liquor….

But Paul knew, of course, that a few drinks improved his driving. Now, if he could get a little closer… "Please! Please, Paul! Slow down!" the girl begged again. "Who cares who gets there first?" But he was in no mood to heed her - he was enjoying himself. His BMW was just the car that could beat that Jap car in front. Then, without warning, it happened.

Completely unexpected, a car came up the hill toward them, and a reflex action made Paul pull to the left. Too late, he knew he had gone too far. Desperately he tried to correct it, but he was far too late. The last thing he remembered was total blackness, headlights shining on nothing. And a dreadful feeling of falling.

He became aware he was lying on some rough grass, wondering how he got there. He dimly realised they must've crashed, but he couldn't understand how it was possible to be out of the car and – he experimented with his arms and legs – apparently unhurt. He sat up cautiously, trying to decide what had happened. He was a good driver, wasn't he? Like, better than average, so how could he have done such a thing as run off the road? Hell, he'd only had a few drinks – well, maybe a few more – but he wasn't drunk – well, not very. He found it hard to remember how much – hell, it couldn't have been much – he was perfectly sober now – jeez, it couldn't have been……

His muddled train of thought was interrupted by Moira calling from the far side of the car, now a wreck. The front was demolished back to and including the front doors. He wondered how they could have survived such a prang, but here they were. They must have been thrown clear. Moira looked around in confusion.

"Paul!" she stared wildly at him, "What have you done? Look at the car! Now how do we get home? I knew something was going to happen, the way you were driving…." He tried to put his arms around her, but she pushed him away. "No! Don't touch me! It's all your fault. It wouldn't have happened if you had any sense! I knew you were going too fast, downhill and all..." She started to sob, "Now what will happen?"

Paul tried to collect himself for some sort of defence when he became aware that a car had stopped on the road above them, and two men had come down to the car. Taking absolutely no notice of Paul or Moira, they stood looking. One said in a hoarse whisper, "God, what a mess! They must have been really travelling to have come out this far from the road. Quick, we better see if anyone survived!"

Another voice, mild but authoritative, made Paul turn around to see two more men had seemingly just appeared. They were relaxed but very much under control. One said, "Take no notice of these two; they are trying their best, but there's nothing they can do. We're sorry we didn't get here sooner, but then you weren't expected, you see." Moira shook his arm and pointed to the car, "Something terrible happened. I don't understand…"

"Yes, young lady, but that is why we came. Nothing can happen while we're here. We've come to meet you and help you get settled in. We'll take you to our little village where you might meet others like yourselves."

Paul stood for a few moments trying to get to grips with what had happened. They had crashed badly, disastrously, but here they were, standing in the company of two men who talked incomprehensibly. It was all …. Unreal somehow, particularly as there was not a mark on him.

"Yes, I imagine you would be a bit confused until you get to know what's going on. I'm Thomas, and my friend is John." John standing beside him, smiled and gave a little bow. "Now, we'd better be on our way. We are taking you to our little village." He gently took Moira by her elbow and, as Paul saw it, levitated. John lifted him as well. Bewildered by this time, all they could do was allow themselves to be taken. Where? They hadn't the faintest idea. Moira was the first to recover enough to ask. "Could we get to a phone, do you think? I want to call my mother, to tell her…"

"I'm afraid that isn't possible," Thomas cut her off softly. "You see, you have left that realm behind you, after that crash. Now, you are, what you call, dead."

The sudden realisation of what had happened hit her, and she screamed. "No! No! I don't want to die! How can I be dead?"

"I'm sorry you are upset," Thomas replied gently, "But you'll find it's not so bad, really."

"Balls!" Paul shouted rudely, "We can't be. Look!" He waved his arms, had a quick thought, and felt between his legs, "I'm complete in every way! I can't be dead!"

"Yes, we know just what you're going through, and that's why we're here."

"You said just now that you'd come to meet us. How the hell can that be? We've only just had the crash! How could you know?" "It's all strange, I know," Thomas replied, "but believe me, I know what you're going through. It might seem only a few minutes since your crash, but in fact, it's been quite some little time – your time, that is. Well, we're here! Come let's go inside."

While Thomas had been talking, neither Paul nor Moira were conscious of any surroundings; they seemed to be in a fog, dismal and dark. They had left the crash, and now there was a cottage before them

– no motion, just there. How, they knew not. They were ushered inside to be met by a pleasant-looking woman. "Hello! I am Jessie, one of your welcoming group. Our job is to tell you the things you would like to know, and to try and smooth the sudden transition you've just had…"

"OK then," Paul interrupted rudely, "Tell us where we are supposed to be!" Moira joined in, "Is this heaven?"

"It really depends on your point of view," Jessie answered, smiling. "We are in one part of the realms of Spirit very similar to the Earth-plane, often called the Astral Plane." Paul would have none of that. "Where are all the angels?" he said truculently. "Harps? All that crap..." Thomas interrupted gently. "Easy, lad, easy! We know you don't understand, but remember you've just arrived." "From what I see," Paul was lost, bewildered, and angry. "This is like any other place – rooms like any others, furniture, tables, and chairs…." He looked down at his body, unable to accept what Jessie had said. He stretched his arms, and thumped his chest, "It's real! Look at me! I'm complete! How can I be dead! I bet if I go looking for a phone, I'll find one!" And, on an impulse, he headed for the door. "I'm off to find it!" Moira reached out to stop him, but Jessie touched her arm. "John will keep an eye on him – he'll come to no harm."

John nodded and disappeared just like that. Jessie saw how shocked Moira was at seeing that and smiled. "It's alright! Don't be alarmed. That sort of thing is quite normal here. There's quite a bit to explain, as you can see. Sit down and relax a little. Would you like a cup of tea?"

Moira nodded dumbly. What? Tea in Heaven? By this time, she was past more surprises and sat in the chair indicated, while Jessie sat opposite.

Another woman came in, as if on cue, with a teapot, cups, and other things on a tray. This was so homelike that Moira started to feel a little more comfortable under the gracious attention of Jessie and her companion.

She poured the tea, handed a cup to Moira, and then said, "Now, take your time and tell us what happened." Moira, glad of the chance, started with a rush, "I knew he was driving too fast…." Jessie held up her hand, "Take it easy! Not so fast! Just take your time now, from the beginning."

Moira took a deep breath and started again. "We were going home over the ranges when Paul – he's my fiancé – was driving too fast trying to catch the car ahead. He had been drinking and wouldn't listen! It all happened so fast, I'm not sure, really, but I think he tried to dodge another car, lost control, and ran off the road. We must have dropped a long way!" She stopped, reliving that awful moment as they plunged through space. She started sobbing, and Jessie leaned forward and took her arm. The girl went on, "It was terrible! I don't really know what happened then, but I got up some time later- I don't know how long- and found Paul standing looking at the car. It was wrecked. So how are we able to be here now? I mean, what are we if we're dead? But we're complete! Paul's right about that!" She held up her hand. "How can this be?" She waved it about, "How can I have a hand, and how can I enjoy this cup of tea when my body must be smashed up? How is it that I still have a body?" she cried in distress.

"Yes, we have bodies," Thomas grinned, "And it must be quite a surprise. What would help you, though, is for you to ask a few questions, and then we can explain things better, perhaps. First, what are your beliefs about life and death?"

"I suppose, "Moira paused to collect her thoughts, "I always believed I would go to Heaven," she hesitated, "But I really don't know. You see," She felt a little more confident, "There seem to be several ideas about. While I was at University, I went to a lecture given by one of the psychologists who said that according to the best authority, there was no possible way anyone could survive after death, because there was nothing that could survive. I think he meant there was no soul. I know everyone's afraid of death – so am I, but then… I don't know now." She looked at the faces waiting with friendly support, fully understanding her feelings.

"Then, for a while, I went along with some Christians, who said if I believed in Jesus Christ, he would take away all my sins, and I would go to Heaven." She paused, more bewildered than ever. "But they said there would be angels and harps and things. Where are they? And where do I go to be judged?" Jessie hastened to comfort the now distraught girl.

"It's not like that, dear child, not like that at all! It's going to be alright. I promise you!" Thomas added gently, "Yes, we know it is taught on the Earth-Plane, and mostly they've got it quite wrong! Now, one more question, and this might point you in the right direction. Do you believe in the human spirit?"

"I don't know! I don't think I know anything anymore!" She sobbed, "You don't think about it, do you? I've never thought about dying, not at my age! I still find it hard to believe!" Jessie collected the sobbing girl into her arms, giving her silent comfort.

"Leave it for now," she said softly, "You've been through enough for now. I think perhaps you should rest now for a while. We can talk later. After all, we've plenty of time…" Moira recovered enough to ask, "What happened to Paul? I'd like to see him if just to give him another rocket!"

"Don't worry about him – John's got him under his care, and they'll be back in a little while." She rose and held out her hand. "Come on, let's get you settled for a good rest."

Moira reluctantly decided to go along; she could do little else but trust them. A brief reflection, and she knew she was perfectly safe. Also, she realised how drained she was.

Jessie led the way along a perfectly normal passage, doors along the way to a nice-looking room complete with a comfortable bed, a little vanity, windowed with tasteful curtains. She sighed with relief as Jessie laid her down, drew a quilt over her, and she knew nothing more as she drifted off into a deep sleep.

Rebellion

Paul paused in indecision as he reached the street. Which way? To the left? He thought they might have come from that direction, but he was only guessing. That was when he noticed something odd about the light. It had been around midnight when they crashed, and dark, of course. Now, he realised that it was nearly as dark, not daylight, but not night either. And sometime later – how much? – the light had not changed. There was a dreamlike luminescence with no shadows. Something else to find out about. He started off to the left but had not gone far when he thought he had made a mistake, for the cottage he thought was there was gone, and it had grown much darker. He seemed to be in a fog; nothing was clear, only some darker patches. With no landmarks, he was lost. Feeling strong déjà vu and the beginning of panic. He turned around, totally disoriented.

"Paul! Wait!" He turned in relief toward the voice but was slightly peeved to find he had been followed.

"You'd gone further than I thought! And I promised to look after you!"

"Look after me?" Paul tried to bluster, but John knew better. "If you really want to stay out here, you can – you're a free man – but I strongly advise against it." Paul wanted to know why.

"See that dark patch over there? Over there are nasties you wouldn't believe. It's dangerous!"

"Dangerous?" Paul spoke with a belligerence he didn't really feel. "Yes, dangerous for a newcomer like yourself. You can find out the hard way if you like, but I strongly suggest you get to know about this new life you're just starting before you wander off. So come along! I promised to look after you, and we're going back." He took Paul's arm, but he stood stubborn.

"Thomas said I'm dead!" Paul shouted. "Don't be so prickly," John said calmly, "Yes, you're dead, and so am I. I died, just as you did, as we all did, here…"

"But I can't be dead!" Paul shouted, "Look, I have my whole body! I'm alive! I see you, you see me…" He stopped and groaned, "I must be dreaming! I guess I'll wake up soon…"

"You're confused, alright, but you're not alone; almost everyone, when they arrive like you – unexpectedly, by accident – feels the same. That's where we come in, to try to get you over the first hump or two." Paul considered that for a few moments, then shook his head.

"No!" he said doggedly, "It's not what they said! They said when you die, you sleep for ages, until the sound of the last trumpet or something. I remember them talking about it at school. Then you were woken up and would be resurrected. This," he waved his arms about, "is nothing like that. Anyway, I never believed any of that religious crap, and also, I don't know whether to go along with the shrinks when they say we are only advanced animals, that we come from mud, and we return to it, and that we're finished! Kaput! Finito! - when we die." He shrugged and shook his head, "I don't know anything anymore!"

"Come with me; I want to show you something. If we can find it, that is." "Find what?"

"Something that might help to show you what happened to you, That is, if you want to?"

Paul had to ask. "What are we looking for?" John grinned, "Evidence. Come on!"

That was enough for him, so off they went in what Paul was sure was the wrong direction. John said cheerfully, "That way is a very nice way! On the other hand, many like to go that way!" He turned and pointed behind them. Paul felt John was just being funny, but something tugged at his memory, something about a yellow brick road, though the connection escaped him.

The easy, relaxed friendliness of John was something a little difficult for Paul. He had always felt a little uncomfortable with strangers; he didn't trust them. He had found that when you did, you were a candidate for being done yourself. He didn't know it, of course, but his own attitude was the main cause of this, for he always had his eye out for the Main Chance, and if he could get a little further up the heap than anyone else, he did. That's what it was all about, wasn't it? Eat or be eaten. Take him for a sucker if you can, because if you don't, he'll do you! He didn't get where he was by being Mr. Nice Guy. He had fought for everything he owned, including the car he loved. It was his most prized possession. With it, he had Status. He wondered if it was possible to see it.

"That's where we're heading," John picked up his thought.

"It might give you a better idea of what happened. Now from here, you are the guide. You know just where it happened."

"Yes, but," Paul was puzzled. "How can we go there? I mean, if this is Heaven or some other outlandish place…."

"First, this isn't quite Heaven, and it isn't quite Hell either. It's a bit hard to explain without having a bit of background, but you'll catch on. Just accept what you find for a start."

While they were talking, John was leading him back through the dark patch he had warned about, but to Paul's surprise, and he realised later, his disappointment - nothing happened to them. The reason for that was not to appear for a long time.

They emerged from the dark patch into a slightly brighter area; there were buildings, streets, and people. Paul started to recognise the area, and then there was the hill before them.

"Down there!" he pointed excitedly, "it'll be down there!" In a moment, they stood on the site, but Paul was further puzzled. He was sure it had not been very long since they shot into blackness, to finish up here in a mangled heap. There were signs of broken bushes, and a hole gouged out of the turf, but no car. Hell, it could only have been an hour or two…

"I know what you mean," John answered his unspoken thought, "But we don't work to the same time scale here. It means little to us. But if you want to know, we can find out."

Paul was fairly sure where to look for the car, and they found it without any trouble. A quick glance inside was all he needed.

John led a shocked Paul into the little office, where they discovered it was four days after the event. Still numb with shock at seeing the wrecked car, all the implications, and all the trauma, he was further upset by John, who seemed to walk right through the corner of the desk. It was then he noticed there was a vague unreality about what he had known in the real world. There was a mistiness, a lack of substance in the walls, floor, and the view from the window. In a rising sense of loss, he looked about the world he had known, the world in which he had grown up and which was now unreachable. He felt totally bewildered and hopeless, unable to make sense of any of it, and stood, angry and frustrated at the fate which had dealt him this cruel blow.

He had lost everything, his status, possessions, his girl, his lovely car. It was strange, he thought dimly, that in the process of all this, he had not worried the least that he had lost his life.

He looked at the man at the desk and tried to get his attention. He tried banging the desk, and his hand went straight through. In his frustration, he swung at him, and the same thing happened; his hand went through as if nothing was there. Almost crying with anger, he raged around the office, attempting to scatter papers, file cabinets, and telephones. But he could touch nothing. The man at the desk took absolutely no notice of him. John tried to calm him.

"Paul! Paul! Take it easy! You'll find things aren't nearly as bad as you think right now!"

"Why can't I touch him? And all the other stuff? I can see them. Can't I? There he sits, taking no notice!"

"Well, you see, he can't," John replied with his little smile. "We're on a different wavelength from all this now." He waved around the room. "He can't see you because he can see only with his body's eyes, and he doesn't know how to use his inner vision; you can bet!" Paul snorted with disgust.

"That means I can't even be a ghost! There are a few people I'd like to haunt…"

"Let's be getting back now, if that suits you?"

He realised there was no point in hanging about and shrugged in half-hearted agreement. Then he remembered he hadn't eaten for a long time, it seemed. He was tired, hungry, and churlish, in a situation completely beyond his control. "Food if you want it," John answered. "All the food you can eat when we get back, and here we are!"

In a mind-wrenching flick, they were there. Just a blur – just as quick as a blink. It was very disconcerting, suddenly dashing about like this, literally as quick as a blink. The most staggering thing so far was how real things were here, down to complete bodies, breathing air, feeling hungry, and he was starting to feel tired, as well. All this was totally unexpected, but he was forced by what he had just seen, to accept he was indeed dead. He wondered if someone was trying to delude him in some way, but why? It made no sense. Back at the house, he looked around for Moira.

"She's sleeping," Jessie answered his unspoken thought, "She needed a good rest, to help her over the shock of arrival. I guess you could do with resting too, but would you like a snack first?"

"I just don't get it!" Paul shook his head, "We're supposed to be dead, or so you all tell us, so how come we need food? I thought…. Oh, I don't know anything anymore!"

"We know exactly what you're going through, and that's our job to help you get used to the idea, so to speak." Jessie laughed, "This is the halfway house, something like the ones the French used in World War Two, helping Allied airmen back to safety. Only instead of enemy Germans, there are other nasties out there."

"We try to ease the shock as much as we can, particularly for such as yourselves, arriving in an accident – any sudden unexpected death. We get as many as we can, but we can't meet them all. So, make yourself comfortable. There is food coming shortly. Don't be surprised – the way it works is that if you think you need food, then you need food. Most of us don't bother much, but it's nice to sit down with some good company sometimes."

"Ok. Good, and thanks... But tell me, where are we? Is this Heaven? I want to know. Is this Heaven or the Other Place? I haven't believed in either, but if you insist we're dead, it must be one or the other!"

"It's a bit difficult to explain," Jessie looked thoughtful. "There are no places, really. What most people believe in, as actual places, are no more than states of existence. Heaven can be on Earth; so can Hell. There are no such things in the biblical sense; no golden streets, no angels with harps, no heavenly choirs – I think you'd be bored stiff with a diet of that!"

"It's more as if you're happy and everything's going fine; you could say you're in Heaven. The same with the other; there are many on Earth living in awful misery, with no comfort, no love. That would be hell, I think."

"Ok then, but where are we?" Paul insisted. At that moment, a girl entered with a tray. She was wearing a Grecian gown of some beautiful, radiant green substance that set off her golden face and arms to perfection. "I suppose you're Greek, and your name's Diana," Paul said with a little snort.

"Don't be so touchy!" she said softly as she put her hand on his arm. He started to pull away but found her touch reassuring. She went on with friendly concern in her voice. "Of course, this is all strange…"

"Hell," Paul exclaimed, "everyone's going around telling me it's strange! Of course, it's bloody strange! Tell me something else, why don't you?" The girl took his outburst, continuing to smile, and when he stopped, feeling foolish, she went on as if nothing had happened.

"We can help, if you will let us." She guided him to the table, "You might feel better if you eat something." She offered him a plate of sandwiches. "This might keep you going for a little while."

He allowed her to sit him down and accepted a sandwich and cup of coffee, both delicious, he noted. But he could not get used to these things. Food and drink when you're dead? He sat, trying to gather his bruised ego into something like his usual self; slightly supercilious and intolerant, often rude whenever he didn't have to toady to the boss; there was always a boss somewhere. He ate, feeling self-conscious as the others watched him, albeit with friendly concern, a thing he had seldom met before. This brought a sudden, unexpected up-welling feeling of loss, his lifestyle, his car, and his yuppie future ruined. All gone because of his stupidity, that bloody silly race. All gone, he realised bitterly.

Death was supposed to be final, and here he was – dead. Or so they kept telling him. A hand on his shoulder made him sit up.

"Come on, have something more to eat." The girl pushed the plate towards him. "That's another thing," he thought disgustedly, "How did I know her name?" She looked at him with a little smile.

"We speak to each other if we want to, but we don't need to…" "You mean telepathy?" Paul asked, disbelieving, "That's all hogwash! Well, isn't it?" He finished defensively. Diana looked at him with her little grin tugging away at the corners of her mouth, saying nothing. He looked back in astonishment.

"You just said …" he hesitated, sorting out his thoughts, "That you were indeed born in Greece around the time of Plato!"

"That's right," she answered. "So, it does work. But have no fear," she hastened to add. "We cannot enter your mind if you don't want it. We can only read what you send to us. Your difficulty is that you don't realise that you're sending your thoughts to others. On the Earth-plane, it happens all the time, but nobody notices it because it usually gets masked by a hundred other things, and besides, your culture says it doesn't happen. Here you must learn to keep your thoughts to yourself, if only because if you do not, the whole place will get cluttered with all kinds of rubbish!"

All this he realised; he understood without exchanging a word. He was also intrigued by her modern mode of expression. She laughed.

"Just a matter of being in contact with all you modern types!"

What really did puzzle him was that everything he discovered, created further mysteries, like all the top academics on Earth said that the centre of intelligence of man was the brain. Well, here he was, knowing everything he ever knew back there – and a lot more besides – and his brain had been destroyed in the crash.

For all that and all they were telling him, he was still bothered by a dearth of facts. He had died – correction, his body had – but he still had just one, just like the one he had before. And this one was complete, even to several teeth lost in a brawl in rugby. He was aware of his surroundings; he could think things through, more or less, and he had communicated by pure thought. Why did he feel so ignorant? Unknowns everywhere.

And the only way he was going to find out was to swallow his pride and ask. He turned to Thomas, and asked, still peeved.

"Exactly where is this astral world in relation to Earth?"

"I must answer with a question of my own." He paused, thoughtful. "Do you know anything about physics? The construction of matter, that stuff?"

"Not one of my strong points," Paul shrugged, "Money, yes. Physics, too tough for me!"

"Ok then, we'll be basic," Thomas replied. He knew better than to lecture or sound too learned or pompous. "It's a matter of frequency, wavelength, vibration, or whatever term you understand best – they all mean the same, roughly. All matter, whether here, or on Earth, is vibrating at a particular rate depending on the plane you're relating to. It's a bit like radio signals; on Earth, you're constantly being bombarded by hundreds of radio signals, day and night. Your body does not detect them – you don't know they're there without a radio set, tuned to the frequency you want to receive. You only get one station at a time, the one you're tuned to. That's because they are all on different frequencies, and we select the one we want. If you get all at once – all together – it's what a radio engineer calls white noise. All signals together, and you can't separate one from another."

"Maybe, perhaps, we have the same thing here: I've never thought about it. We do know, though, that each realm is separated from others by the same thing – vibration. Each one – and there are more than most people know about – is vibrating at a different rate. The lowest is the Earth-plane, the Moon, planets, and so on. We, here, are a little above that rate. And as you know, all radio signals occupy the same space, and so with the higher realms. To go back to the Earth-plane, for instance, we must retune to speak. That's what John did when he took you back, just now. And as you will learn, there are many realms higher than this. The higher the realm, the finer the fabric, and the higher you must tune to reach, and for the most part, most people cannot see even as high as this level because Earth people are too physically bound to see it. It also means that we, here, cannot see much of the level above us, let alone go there. It is entirely a matter of your own level of progress, and your views toward others, mainly."

"So? How come I have a body then, if it's not made of – er – what did you say?"

"Basic Earth material will do," Thomas answered. "Remember, on Earth, everybody – nearly everybody that is, sees things only within the range of their body's eyes and not as you are now. Only a few can see with their inner or spiritual eyes, and some learn by training."

"So, what's this body made of, then?" Paul insisted.

"Look around you!" Thomas waved his hand about. "Everything here is made of the same stuff, even you! We call it the Etheric Force – some call it the God Force…"

"Here we go!" Paul shouted, jumping to his feet. "I wondered when you'd get around to the God stuff! You're all the same! Where's your Bibles? Why aren't you wearing a dog collar?" Paul snorted in disgust. "I've never heard such a load of bullshit!" He finished his outburst to see the others, Jessie, Diana, Thomas, and John regarding him, little smiles on the faces around him. But even Paul, in his blindness, could see there was little amusement: there was genuine concern.

He felt embarrassed and a little foolish and sat down; Thomas continued calmly. "I know we will not get very far now; you are tired and need a rest. Also, you will be happier in a group, much more like yourself. In fact, all newcomers go to the place most suited to their outlook and character, where they would be most comfortable. Only you can decide on this. We can only guide you."

Paul sat in silent thought for a few moments as he tried to catch up with it all. There was far too much to swallow in one gulp. And for all his arrogance, even rudeness, he realised through the fog he was in, that these people were calm, friendly, and what he could not understand was their genuine desire to help. No words were needed – it showed.

He took a deep breath. "Alright then," he shrugged. "How do I get to this place? And if I go, what will I find?"

"You'll find others much like yourself, I expect. How to get there? You just go out the door and follow the path you see there. But. I strongly advise you to get some rest, and take time to think about it a little," Thomas continued, "Yes, well, John said when you were out a little while ago, that there were unpleasant places out there. Is that where I'm going? You said I had a choice. What is it like there?" He was not making sense, but he got his message across.

Thomas replied, "What you need to know is that the door you've just passed through – the door from Earth life – to this – changes nobody. Everybody that comes here, and that means everybody, arrives the same person they were on Earth. A good guy remains a good guy, while a sadist, brute, rapist, murderer – any kind of villain you know about – and some you don't – comes here without any change. A few confess their sins, receive absolution, and so on, may be better off, if they are really genuine. There are different rules here, as you will learn. So, you will meet them all, if you choose that place. You can get along, but it will be tough."

"But I'm not a criminal or anything like that!" Paul protested. "I've always kept within the law! Well – mostly! I'm not a bad guy, really!"

"That may be," Thomas frowned, "But that is only a small part of it. Thinking you're good is no measure of your worth, as you will learn. I'm sorry to keep saying this, but it's a great pity that almost every newcomer to these realms arrives so ignorant of what it's all about here. You must learn if you want to get anywhere."

Paul, however, was much more interested in finding out more about the other places. Were they like Earth, where one might live in a city dominated by the Mob or some other criminal organisation, barely aware of their presence? Or did hard-bitten bruiser types run things? Thomas told him it depended on where he was. There were places close to normal Earth-plane in all ways, but there were others – places to avoid. Most definitely!

"But as I said," Thomas went on, "You are free to go wherever you wish."

Paul looked around the group feeling strange, somehow. They were all relaxed, friendly, and in no way pushy or domineering. His sneering tones made no impact on them, and he slowly realised how much of an ungrateful yokel he had been since his arrival. He had never felt like this before, nor had he met people like this, so undemanding it was not natural!

John broke his mood. "We hate to say this again, but you'll learn, and I might add you're doing fine, and before you go off the deep end again, I am not patronising!" He could see Paul gritting his teeth. "We're your friends, not the opposite! What might be some help right now is a little question. Since you arrived, have you felt as if you've been here before this?"

Paul gave a little grimace, "I don't think so - not that - hang on! When we were out just now, I had this queer feeling just before you caught up with me. Was that it?"

"Did you feel, "Diana asked, "As if you'd been here, maybe in your dreams?"

"Well …I …I dunno! That's all bunk, isn't it? You know, travel while you're asleep, all that guff?"

Jessie nodded, "That's what most people think. In fact, many come here in their sleep – Astral Travel, some people call it. Then one day, they die and come here permanently. The 'dreams' often prepare you for life here. Now, I'm sure you'll find it very nice here." She stood up, "It's time you had a rest and gave yourself some time to settle your thoughts. Diana will show you where to go."

He decided he could do little else but go along with this, and feeling more relaxed; he followed Diana along a passage to a small room with two unoccupied beds. She closed the door behind her leaving him to realise he was tired. He lay down and was immediately in a deep, dreamless sleep.

Runaway

Sometime later, how much he had no way of knowing, Paul awoke, disorientated. He looked out the window and saw nothing but some sad-looking trees. For a few moments, he had no recollection of previous events, how he came to be in a strange room. He wondered what time it was and why he had not gone to work.

Then it all came tumbling back. He was supposed to be dead. He had been asleep, he thought, and dreaming, he thought and wondered if he could dream if he were already dreaming. He must have needed that sleep, however, for he was much refreshed without waking up feeling grotty.

All was quiet, but there was a murmur of voices somewhere down the passage. He started down the hallway wondering where Moira had got to. Just as he passed a door, it opened, and there she was. She had been crying and looked like a mess. He wondered if she would be like that if they had married. She looked at him, surprise and shock in her face. He started to put his arm around her, but she coldly pushed him away. Puzzled, not realising she had received his unkind thought, he asked, "Hey, what's the matter?"

"It's just as well we're not married, don't you think?" She brushed past him and went along to the large room they had been in when they arrived. He followed, now knowing he had put his foot right in it but determined to brazen it out. "Aw, Moira, you know I didn't mean that!" He realised he'd better keep a sharp watch on his thoughts in the future. She turned on him. "Yes, you'd better be more careful, but it doesn't matter too much; it's too late for that, don't you think? I can see we'd never have made it, now that I've seen how you behaved last night. So, consider us no longer engaged!" She crossed to the other side of the room, sat down, and glared at him. He started toward her.

"No! Keep away! I want nothing more to do with you! Don't you know what you've done?" Her voice rose in pitch and volume, "Don't you know you've just got us killed, you and your clever driving! Your arrogance! You're too much a smart-alec! You always were a show-off, too much to say, and far too much to drink...." She subsided, sobbing, her face in her hands.

He stood, shocked into silence by her outburst, dimly aware that she had some justification, but hell, he had been doing only what everyone did. Well, didn't he? You have a few drinks and enjoy yourself. Sometimes, no, mostly, they scraped through. That is, mostly. He felt aggrieved by her attitude. She was hysterical, that's all.

Her attitude crystallized his half-formed desire to stay in this realm. It should be good fun, with no restrictions, as John had hinted, and no more nagging women, telling him to slow down when he knew perfectly well how to drive. Well, didn't he? He shrugged. Well, maybe he misjudged that corner that prevented him from regaining control. But as he stood there, he knew, without any doubt, it had been his actions alone that had brought them here. "To hell with it!" he thought. "Too late to worry about it now! Anyhow, I'm off!" He also realised Moira had received all of that, so, with no further need for talk, he turned and, with a defiant wave, was off through the door. Outside, he ran, before he could change his mind. Taking the first path he could see, he took off with no idea, of course, where he was heading.

In a short distance, it seemed, there was nothing in sight.

Surprised, he turned around, thinking he had mistaken his direction, but there was nothing there. He shook his head in puzzlement. Surely, he hadn't come so far so soon. He looked about for some sign of life, buildings, or people. Nothing, except for a few scrawny trees and some low shrub-like stuff. There was only this path. There was little option but to follow it; it had to lead somewhere.

Dimly aware that it was getting darker as he went, he thought it must be getting close to evening, and he would need to find a place to spend the night. The few people he saw quickly scampered out of sight as he approached. Then, among the trees was a large building. Feeling a bit like an explorer, he slowly ventured closer, and could soon read the large sign on the front: -

ALL GUNS, SWORDS, KNIVES BANNED; CASH ONLY, NO IOU'S

With a snort of disbelief, he went a little closer. As he approached the front door, a body came flying out, to land in a heap almost at his feet, and a large man wearing an apron appeared at the door, shouting.

"Get out! Lizard turd! Scum! And don't come back!" He stood glaring at the wretch, who cowered away, scrambled to his feet, and scuttled out of sight around the corner. The publican went back inside, leaving Paul wondering at the wisdom of following him in. After that demonstration, he was not sure. Standing there undecided, two other men came along, chatting together, went right past him and on inside, so he went in after them. Inside was a large bar room, a long bar with well-stocked shelves behind. He started toward the bar feeling for his wallet, and stopped in embarrassment. It was not there. The barman – the big man he had seen at the door – saw him stop. "What's wrong, mate? You want a drink, or don't ya?" "I've lost my wallet, I think."

He felt in his pockets again, feeling foolish. "I'm sure I had it a while ago…" "New arrival, eh?" the man sneered. "We get 'em all here!" Paul felt aggrieved. "Yes, I am, as it happens."

"It happens, alright!" growled the barman, "All the time, it happens! You bums always arrive without any money!" Paul tittered, snorted, and giggled and then full laughter, although he knew it was not at all funny. It was more hysteria than mirth. He HAD to be dreaming! "What's so damned funny then?" demanded the barman. "Well, it's true! All you guys come here without any money and demand free beer!"

"I'm not laughing at that!" Paul protested, "It's what you said. Of course, people arrive here without money! They've just died, haven't they? How do you think they would have any money?"

"Don't you get smart with me, you squirt!" He leaned menacingly. "You better be more polite here. If you get my drift!" A quick look around the bar quickly reinforced that thought. At his laughter, they had looked up at him, and there were some fearsome types among them. Several looked as if they'd come straight from Sherwood Forest, one or two Cavaliers, even a group of Romans, soldiers, or gladiators; he wasn't sure.

Then a fight broke out between some red coats and some other roughnecks, and they meant business. The barman leapt over the bar, shouting, "Knock it off, you scum! Knock it off, I say!" He completely ignored a chair intended for someone else smashed over his head. He grabbed the two nearest and banged their heads together. And then two more got the same treatment. "Now, you bloody layabouts! Who's going to pay for the damage? Let's see...three chairs, one table, and one tankard - that comes to...three sovereigns. I guess. OK, then, who's going to pay?" He stood glaring at them.

One red coat spoke up. "You know we ain't got that kind of stuff!" "Yes, I know! You useless toe-rags come in here, wreck the joint, and can't pay your way!" "It wasn't our fault!" the one who had spoken first said, "It was those yellow bas..." As he spoke, the other parties in the fracas lunged forward. "Call us cowards..." "Shut up! Shut up! The bleedin' lot of you! One more peep, and you're for it! Now, who's going to pay?"

The erstwhile combatants shuffled their feet. "OK, then, get out, the lot of you useless pack of no-hopers! And don't come back without three sovereigns! Now, get out. Before I throw you out!" He stood, glaring at them as they scowled at him and each other, muttering darkly over their lost beer.

As peace returned, Paul decided he'd better try to butter up the barman. It could be to his advantage. He might talk him into a loan. He asked, "Does that happen very often? Fights, I mean?"

"All the time!" The barman growled as he returned behind the bar, "This bloody lot don't do nothin' else! Those Romans" He nodded in their direction, "Those bloody Romans! Always looking for a fight! I'm just damn' glad they didn't mix in with this last lot! I dunno why I put up with any of them. I never liked the coppers much, but now we could use them here!"

"You mean there are no police here?" Paul was interested. He was generally law-abiding - well, as much as most law-abiding people, but the idea of no-one to check up on him excited him. He well knew that there had been only one law recognised in his circle; namely, thou shall not get caught! And time and effort spent on the barman might pay. The fact that he needed money, after all, made it all the more necessary to become organised, to arrange, or to find out how, one might obtain a supply of the stuff.

However, he was not going to ask, straight out, for money. That was much too crude, too much like begging. He had to work out a strategy, a way of putting the barman in his debt. Fortunately, the barman was busy and gave Paul time to think of something. For the present, he was being ignored, and that should have been fine, but he was bereft of any ideas. He regretted, briefly, leaving the haven, wondering if he could find his way back. No, he wouldn't do that! That would be surrender; No way!

A bottle hurtling past his ear decided things for him. This was no place to be. He headed for the door, dodging more bottles, tankards, and even bodies. It appeared useless hanging about here. He reluctantly went outside. He thought maybe he could wait until things cooled inside, but there was no sign of that. Anyhow, he would crawl to no-one!

Capture

Feeling a bit dejected, he wandered off, not caring where he went. He smarted under the injustices of being killed, arriving in this place; hell, he HAD to get some money! But there was no-one to write him a cheque when he was a bit short, no-one to turn to without losing what was left of his self-esteem. That had already taken a beating when Moira turned away from him.

Down a faint path, he went, not aware that he very quickly left the tavern behind. However, the path must go somewhere, although it seemed to head into a much darker area than where the pub was. He could feel it getting more dismal. Where Thomas and the others had been was much more pleasant.

There was the odd shadowy figure, but every time he got closer, they melted away out of sight, afraid of him. Then there was a rustle behind him. He turned, but he was far too slow. Two great hulking figures bore him to the ground, pinning him there. One of them growled, "Give us your valuables, and be quick about it!" Paul gave a short bark. "I've got nothing, nothing at all! It's no good robbing me!" "Turn out your pockets then! Come on, quit stalling!" He did as ordered, but protested, "It's no good, I tell…" He was silenced by a blow on the jaw. "Shut up, or I'll shut you up!" The other growled, "It's no good, Bert; he ain't got nothin'." The first man gave Paul a mighty push, snarling, "Just our bloody luck! Come on; we've wasted enough time round 'ere! Let's move on." And the two muggers disappeared among the straggling trees. Paul lay where he was for a little while, gathering his scattered wits.

He discovered more mysteries. Oh, yes, you can get mugged, but he expected that, after seeing what went on in the tavern. No, it was when you get a poke on the jaw; it should be sore. Not so! He felt it, but it was just like it usually was. Something else to ponder over.

He carefully picked himself up, looking cautiously about. With nobody in sight, he started down the track again, this time trying to watch behind as he went. And it paid off. He was sure he was being followed again and, after a few yards, decided he'd better duck. Just in time! Two dark figures - not the same ones - came along, looking for a likely victim. They both carried clubs and looked very mean and nasty. Paul hid behind a tree, trying to look like one. He must have succeeded, for the pair kept going, passing him without a sideways glance.

Once again relieved, he stayed where he was until he was sure the way was clear. He decided this was tough going. Along with any risk of being jumped, he had absolutely no experience whatsoever of anything away from cities. He was town born and bred and had no love for any of the popular weekend pursuits, tramping, and such. He had once gone skiing with a few friends, but out of the two hours or so spent on skis, he had spent about one hour and fifty-five minutes picking himself up out of the snow. He never went again. His main pastimes were rugby, car races, beer, and girls. All very neat and tidy. He had never risen on a cold morning, lit a fire - he didn't know how – and cooked breakfast.

As he looked around at the dismal scene, he felt, for perhaps the first time ever, alone, lonely, and miserable. He would have enjoyed that beer, and he was starting to feel hungry. Why? He wondered. Why did I have to run off like that? And I'm starting to wish I could find my way back! He tried to retrace his mad plunge into the wilderness but had to stop in utter confusion. He was hopelessly lost.

He knew absolutely nothing that might have helped - no boy-scout tricks, no woodcraft, nothing. If he could just find that tavern!

A voice from his left made him spin around. An unsavoury-looking creature stood there. "Lost your tongue, have you?" His speech was thick and guttural, in keeping with his miserable appearance. Paul looked at him with distaste, trying to decide whether to ignore him. He would never be seen dead talking to someone like that! Then the irony of that made him snort.

Two strong hands, one on either side, grabbed him from behind. He started to struggle, but a clout on the back of his head showed the futility of that.

"What have we here? Ah! A smart bastard, eh?" as Paul tried to kick backwards at his captors. "We'll have to teach you some manners, won't we?" The biggest of them snarled, "Now, let's get a good look at you!" He grabbed a handful of hair and jerked Paul's head around.

"Aha, A pretty boy! Just what we want, and just what the boss wants! He likes them young" He jerked Paul's hair again, "Come on! You just come along nice and quiet with us. You're a good find. We need some fresh faces." He laughed unpleasantly. "Our entertainment's a bit flat lately. A nice young pretty boy! Almost as good as a girl!"

The implication of that remark took all of Paul's attention for some time. Did they mean what he thought they meant? He quailed at the prospect... suppose it's true? He cursed again his stupidity in not listening to good advice. It looked like costing him dearly.

He was only dimly aware of being dragged over the rough ground, seemingly for hours. All he found out during this was that the big one was called Curly, his mate was Bosh, and the skinny one, not unexpectedly, was Skin. He was also called many other names, much more earthy than that. Paul correctly surmised that this was the norm among the motley gang he had involuntarily joined.

A dim glow ahead showed a dozen or more people, all similar to his captors. He was thrown down before the ugliest man he had ever seen. Big, ugly, unpleasant, and stinking he was.

"Oh ho!" He turned Paul over with a foot clad in rags. "And what do you think you're doing, wandering through our patch? We don't like snoopy strangers here! Are you one of those do-gooders we get prowling about?" He gave Paul a little kick, "No, you can't be one of them. I dunno why, but any time I get near one of them, they disappear. So, who are yer, and wot yer want, alone out here?"

He tried to sit up but was pushed back roughly. "Stay where you are! I don't trust nobody. No how. You can tell me from there!"

"I got lost," Paul muttered

"I can't hear you. Speak up!" A prod from his foot was the last straw. Paul shouted in a mixture of fear, anger, and frustration, "I got lost, I said!"

"Alright! Alright! You don't have to shout. So, you got lost, eh? Where do you think you were going then? Ain't nowhere to go out here! So, where you off to?"

"I was looking for the tavern. I thought it was somewhere around here." He slowly sat up, being careful not to antagonise the ugly one. This time he made it.

The ugly one looked around at his band. "No tavern around here, is there? Curly, you get around; where's the tavern around here?" Curly looked blank for a moment, then he said, "Guess it's that place 'way back that-a-way." He pointed over his shoulder in a direction different from where they had come from, or so Paul thought. But then, he was lost. Curly went on, "It's a bloody long way from here, though. Only been there once. Got chucked out for fighting. Not much of a place anyway."

One member of the gang spoke up. Paul was interested to see a woman - correction - a girl, as he got a better look at her. "Billy, I think he's just arrived. You know, one of these guys that just seems to show up from nowhere. You know the ones." She was probably older than Paul, tall and thin, almost gaunt. She looked youngish, but the more he looked, the less sure he was. She had clear signs of past beauty, probably lost by her present status.

"What's your name, boy, and are you new here?" Paul was starting to recover a little as the intimidating Billy, now moved a few feet away. He looked around the ugly-looking bunch. All were filthy, in rags, and all gaunt and emaciated. His fastidious nature was affronted and repelled. He reluctantly told them how he came to be among them and demanded to be released.

Billy laughed grimly. "Who do you think you are?" "He wants us to turn him loose!" He roared with raucous laughter, "Oh, no, me boyo, you're stayin' here! We need a slave or two. Tie him up, Curly, while we decide how to use him."

Curly and Bosh quickly had him tied hand and foot. He struggled briefly and uselessly, gave up, and tried bravado. "What do you want me for? I'm useless!" Which was quite correct. He had never used his hands for anything other than eating, dressing himself, and sport.

"Well!" Ugly Billy came and stood over him. "Let's see now," He scowled, standing with his chin in his hand. "Let's see just what you're good for." He signalled with his hand. Curly and Bosh, on either side of Paul, picked him up, making him stand, after a fashion. Bosh grabbed Paul's shirt and gave an almighty yank. Off it came as if it were damp paper. Curly followed suit with his trousers, leaving him standing naked. Surprised and shocked, he stood, arms locked behind, unable to cover his lower regions. His uppermost thought was, of course, embarrassment, but several things puzzled him.

First, he was not in the least cold. And second, the clothes he was wearing were identical to his normal Earth-plane attire, sound, strong fabric. Or so he thought. This stuff was as soft as tissue paper and fell away easily. Was this why they were all dressed in rags? He was jerked back to his predicament by a coarse cackle from one of the women.

"Call yourself a man?" she cackled again, a shrill hag-like noise, "he-he, call yourself a man? I've seen little boys with better equipment. Tiny little thing, more like a little cherry! He! He!"

More than ever, Paul bitterly regretted running away from Thomas, John, and the others. They told him he wouldn't like it. They were right. These people were savages, brutal, uncaring, and crude. They all delighted in his attempts to free himself. They pointed at him, screaming with laughter at every move he made. He could stand it no longer. He hopped forward to Billy. The others were laughing too hard to see what he was doing. In a frenzy of fear, anger, and embarrassment, he gave Billy a Liverpool kiss, hard enough to make his own head swim. Billy had been doubled up with mirth, caught the full head-butt, and fell to his knees.

Aghast at his folly, Paul stood motionless as Billy rose. He wasn't smiling. In desperation, Paul lunged forward again, but Billy held him off with one hand, snarled, and with his other hand, cuffed Paul one two three four, backwards and forwards, until Paul's knees began to sag. Billy, with a grin of sadistic joy, struck him with a vicious uppercut, and Paul crumpled at his feet.

Billy towered over him and drew back his foot, but the one who had spoken when he first arrived pushed him back. "No, Billy, can't you see he's had enough! And we asked for it! I'd have done the same thing, in his position. He…" Billy shrugged off her grip on his arm, but she grabbed him again, "What would you do, if you were him?" "I'd kill anyone who laughed at me! Look what he did to me!" He rubbed his head. He's a bloody looney; that's what he is! He'd better keep out of my way, that's all! Or I'll kill him!"

The woman took no notice of Billy's ravings and knelt to Paul. She straightened his legs and arms as she called to the woman who had taunted him about his equipment. "Come on Jane! Help me with him. Let's get him into the shelter." Jane reluctantly helped, looking back at Billy to be sure he would let them move him. Billy did nothing other than glower at them.

"What you want with him, anyway, Eve?" Eve somehow managed a shrug as they dragged him to the crude shelter.

Noises of scuffle, grunts, thumps, and yells came from behind a rock, and Billy and his men went to investigate, leaving the two women alone with Paul.

Between them, they managed to get Paul inside, still bound, still naked, but strangely, not at all sore after the hefty clout on the jaw. He was actually unhurt. Only his pride had been dented. He sat up carefully, but there was no discomfort at all. The one called Jane snorted. "Hm. Got yourself into a nice pickle, ain't ya? Teach you to make Billy mad! It doesn't pay to make him mad! He he! Fancy you giving him a head-butt! That sure took him by surprise. But," she stopped cackling, "You watch him! He's bad news, that one. I dunno why we stick around. S'pose it's because no-one else ever touches us while he's here."

The one with the unlikely name of Eve spoke up. "How long you been here, pretty boy? And I s'pose you got a name?" Paul, still conscious of his nakedness, told his brief story, feeling like anything but his usual poise. All his self-confidence had gone, and he cursed again his stupidity in tearing off as he had. And although he tried to place the blame for that on something, anything, he knew that he alone did it. Thomas had warned him, but he knew better. All he could do now was to see if there was a way to turn this to his advantage. His thoughts were cut off when he realised one of them had asked him where he had come from. When he told them, Eve parroted his speech.

"I come from New Zealand!" she tried to copy him. "Ha! All proper pansy, are we? You'll soon get that bashed out of you here, with this lot!" Paul was surprised by her reaction. He thought he spoke ordinary type English, but his background placed him slightly above the norm, whereas Eve was solid Cockney. Replying to her last remark, he said, "Why do you stay here then, if you don't like it? What keeps you here?"

Jane shrugged, "I dunno! I s'pose there's nowhere else. Anyhow, here's as good as anywhere. Billy's not so bad if you keep out of his way." Paul turned to Eve. "Are you the same? Do you stay here because you want to, as well?" Eve gave a rueful grin. "I guess so.

There's nowhere else to go. It's all pretty bad. I ain't seen anything else since I got here, and that's a while ago now."

He sat thoughtfully for a few moments, then asked, "Do you know you're supposed to be dead? I met a man back there somewhere who told me I was dead, and he took me to where it happened. So, are we all dead here?" Jane gave her raucous cackle, echoing around the dismal glade.

"Dead? Dead you say? Rubbish! Pigs' tit! I dunno what we are, but we're not that! I'm different like, to what I was: I'm never sick now, and I was sick all of the time, before the fire that was."

"Why, what happened?" Paul leaned forward, hoping they might give him a line on what really happened to him. Jane gave a little shake. "I dunno, like I said, before the fire…. I'm over seventy, but do I look it?" Paul had to admit she didn't, for apart from her gauntness and unkempt look, she wouldn't be much older than himself. More mysteries. Everywhere he looked and everything he learned, there were more mysteries.

First, the light, or the lack of it. It wasn't direct sunlight, as there were no shadows. Nor was there any night or day – just this dim pervasion, a little colour, just drab and drabber. There was no hunger or thirst. He felt he could eat something, but it was more from habit than need. And, since he awoke beside his wrecked car, he had not eliminated any waste from his body, liquid or solid.

But he was breathing, so there definitely was air and, therefore, the need to breathe. But when he checked that, he found there was no need to do even that. True, he felt lighter, brighter if he did. But there was no discomfort or need to gasp for breath if he held his breath, perhaps longer than he should have. When he surreptitiously checked his exposed body, he could find no changes other than a scar to his knee from a boyhood mishap – now gone, and a broken tooth, now whole. All this ran through his mind as Eve stood up and muttered.

"'Bout time they showed up! They only went around the corner; I think I'll take a little look." She went to the rock, looked around, and then returned. "Nobody, anywhere out there. Peace at last!"

"Don't be too sure," Jane said darkly. "I don't trust that Billy-boy nor that Bosh. Remember what they did to that little girl who showed up that time?"

"What happened to her?" Paul asked.

"He used her 'til he was sick of her, then gave her to that animal across the river. Buggered her, he did. He's only an animal himself. The world would be a better place without him and his kind!"

"Yes, well." Paul thought it might be best if he tried to butter these two up a little, "I suppose I've done a few things in my time, but never anything like that. Funny, apart from the ones I met when I arrived, I haven't met any decent people - apart from you two, of course. And how about untying me? I can't do you any harm, and I'm not going to run away until I know a bit more. I've already landed in trouble by being too hasty."

"Why, what happened?" They both wanted to know. He told them how he had left the place, Moira and the others, and that they had told him he wouldn't like it much if he did go away on his own. He finished by saying, "And they were right, of course. I thought I would be OK, but now I'm not so sure, what with these hooligans - not you, of course".

To his relief, the women hastened to release him. A little cramped, he stood up, finding as he did that the stiffness disappeared. He was still naked, but he didn't care anymore. He did want to know, however, what he could do now to improve his position. This was the first time he could remember anyone getting the better of him. He had always lived by the idea, "Do it to them before they do it to you." Now, he was receiving the rough edge, not dishing it out. At school, he had the reputation of being callous, heartless, and certainly not generous. The few friends he had were much the same; there was a state of truce between them rather than genuine friendship.

Right now, he thought regretfully, he could use a few friends, and for the first time in his memory, he came to realise that in order to receive real friendship, he had to give it. Much later, he came to recognise this point as the beginning of his true spiritual growth.

Moira's Experience

Moira awoke from a deep, dreamless sleep, feeling fresh and rested but dreamlike and confused. At once, she was happy in some way, while at the same time, very lost.

Why was she not in hospital, after a very bad crash?

What did Paul do, in a drunken stupor, and where was he now?

She was dead, or so they said. But how could that be? This was nothing like the death people always talked about, certainly not what she had expected. But then, what did she expect? Did she think she would sleep until the Last Day, the resurrection, the time of judgement? Was she about to be "marched in" before the judge to receive the verdict, Heaven or Hell? For eternity. For Eternity! She had reached a conflict of ideas and ideology and didn't know anymore what to think. Through all this, there still ran this strong thread of serenity, of peace.

If she had died in that crash, she had most certainly not been wiped out - kaput - as some Earth-bound philosophies would have it. She was here, wherever that was, and she knew she was here. Therefore, if this was indeed death, then she didn't die. The body she now possessed was the same, except for a scar that should be on her left knee. She had fallen off her bike when she was ten and had several stitches in it. It was now gone, as was a slight blemish on her neck.

So, she was dead. Now what? Then she felt a strong pull, an urge. To see her mother. And with no sense of motion, she was there, at her old home, where she had grown up. There was a casket in the lounge heaped with flowers. The room was full of people all dressed in black, all whispering and looking sad. Her mother, weeping silently, her aunts muttering.

"I don't know why Jocelyn let her go out with that no-good Paul! I knew he was nothing but trouble." "I don't know why," whispered the other, "she didn't have the funeral properly in church, much better, don't you think?"

Moving among the throng, Moira tried to attract someone's attention, but they completely ignored her. Her mother failed to see her. Her father was waving his arms about, excited about something. His arm went sliding clean through her hand. This was a far greater shock than when she first realised she was dead. To be so near those she had known all her life and not be recognised, and the atmosphere of gloom and grief was too much. She sobbed, beating her hands on the coffin, screaming at them.

"I'm not dead! Can't you see me? Please, someone, won't you listen!"

Not a flicker of response did she get from any of them, except her youngest sister, who kept looking in surprise in her direction. In desolation, her one wish was that she could really die and not be in this strange state she was in.

After a short service, she went along to the funeral party. Indeed, she found she could do little else. It was as if she was bound to them. She stood with the others at her own graveside as the vicar made noises about:

"We lay our sister to rest, in the sure and certain knowledge of her resurrection, when the trumpet shall sound, and the Dead will be raised incorruptible!"

She stood in wonder at the words. She had reached the point of wry amusement. She had cried herself out in the frustration of not being recognised and was now standing beside the vicar. She could not resist a derisive guffaw at the inanity of his words. How wrong can you get? She had been killed hence the funeral – but she was very much alive. Of that, she was quite sure.

The funeral over, the force which seemed to hold her seemed to abate; she felt she wanted to return to the cottage, now accepting the fact she was in the Spirit realm.

However, although she had to accept it, she still didn't like it. From what she had seen so far, there wasn't much to it. It was drab, colourless, and cheerless. And Paul had no right to end her Earth life. She grew angry as she thought of it. He had no right! She decided to look for him and, on opening her door, found him coming along the passage. Her outburst was followed by Paul rushing off, and that would be the last she would see of him for some time.

"Hullo, Young Lady!" It was Jessie, with her easy, unassuming manner, "You look well rested. How do you feel now that you've had a good sleep?"

Moira, still steaming over Paul, spoke more harshly than she really meant to. "I'm alright, I suppose! Except I didn't want to die! Not yet, anyway."

Jessie smiled. "You must know we get a great many like you, who wish they hadn't died. But I think you might change your mind soon. This is just a half-way house, set up to look after folk like you, who have an instant transition as you did".

"I'm truly grateful for your help. I'm all mixed up, and maybe you know what happens... I've just been to my own funeral. Is that normal, for someone to do that?"

"That depends," Jessie gave her little smile, "It depends on how much grief there is, dragging you back...." "Yes, that's what it was," Moira interrupts, "They pulled me there!"

"Yes, they do!" Jessie continued, "If they only knew, back there, that you are well, and have a new life to live here, there'd be no need for funerals and sadness. Oh, I know they've lost a daughter, but it's only temporary! Sooner than you - or they - think, you'll be together again. That is, if you want to be. If you don't, and some don't, I expect you'll remain friends. Remember, someone said you choose your friends, but you're stuck with your family!" "Well, what happens now? Is this all there is to the Spirit world?"

"Great Heavens, no!" Jessie laughed, "You are in for a real surprise! That is, if you fit, if you feel right there."

"I don't know what you mean," Moira frowned, "If I feel right there?" Jessie explained with a familiar ease that spoke of long practice.

"The entire Spirit Realm is made up of many different zones or levels. The lowest is the closest to Earth, and this is where those folk go, who are very uncaring and crude in their dealings with others, those that are never kind, either by word or deed. The criminals, the brutes, the sadists. But no-one sends them there. They are there simply because they feel more comfortable there than else. But believe me; it's an awful place. It would be the closest to Hell you're likely to find. Remember, they go to the level of their own choice. Not by anyone else's."

"Then there's the strays, who are not bad people, perhaps not so good either, usually ignorant, and seem to want to stay that way. That's right here, where we are now. We position ourselves here, for we can be of the most use here."

"But you, my girl, are off in a few minutes, to the next zone above this. We will know as we approach it whether or not you can go there. If not, you cannot reach it. Only you will know, and only you can learn and grow spiritually, sufficiently, to enter that realm."

This is how it is for all of us. Neither Thomas, John, nor any other can go beyond the realm most suited to them. Shall we go and see?"

Moira looked intently at her, trying to assimilate all of that and wondering if she could trust her. Jessie laughed again as she picked up the thought. "Look at me," she commanded, "look into my eyes!" Now, look into my mind! What do you see?"

Moira did as bidden and said slowly, "I see beautiful gardens, houses, and - and – it's as if I'm going home." She finished in wonder, "Home!"

Jessie acknowledged her recognition of the truth with another of her lovely smiles. "Remember, dear child, nothing can harm you here, or even where Paul has gone..."

"Does that mean he cannot come to any harm, then?"

"No, not quite," Jessie answered wryly, "I doubt whether he will be knowledgeable enough to be aware of that. What he - and most other arrivals here don't know is that this is primarily a realm of Thought. Thought is everything here. All that is needed is some knowledge of how that works, and nothing can harm you."

"For the present, because you are here with us, we are totally safe, even if we go away from this cottage. But, no, to answer your question – I'm afraid he'll find things a little hard, where he went. But remember, he was warned, and he made the choice to go. John is keeping an eye on him, and when Paul is ready, we will lead him out. We can only guide; it must be his choice."

She stood up and extended her hand. "Ready?"

Moira stood up beside her, apprehensive but trusting. Jessie took her hand. "Come!" She led the way outdoors, along a path towards an area of much brighter light. As they walked along, Moira looked in surprise. This was too much like Earth to go unremarked. "A good reason for that," Jessie replied, "is to reduce as much as possible the shock of passing, for those that come here know the least about themselves and don't seem to want to." She noticed Jessie could have called them the ignorant ones, but she was kinder than that. "They settle in here much easier than if it were a strange setting, and as well, they can be reached easier in a place like this."

As she spoke, Moira noticed that there had been a lifting of the general gloom and a brightening overall with more trees, a few flowers, and even a bird or two. And then an expression of anticipation, of concealing a surprise, stole over Jessie's face. Moira had to ask herself just where they were going, as Jessie's excitement was contagious. "We're nearly there! Just a few more steps!"

That's all it took. A few more steps and the entire scene changed. Everything became almost dazzling, and they were surrounded by beauty, flowers of unbelievable colours, and birds tame enough to touch. And music. Soft ethereal music, which swelled when she reached to touch a flower, the music somehow emphasising the colour, and matching it exactly.

Moira stood with mouth agape in utter astonishment. Slowly turning, she was so stunned by what she saw she murmured a long-drawn-out sigh, "Oh......What is this place? This must be Heaven! Look at all those wonderful flowers! The trees! Oh, and the lovely houses...." She fell silent as she tried to take it all in. There was beauty everywhere, a blaze of colour of every possible hue and tint, many beyond her wildest imaginings, as well as familiar - and unfamiliar -shape, size, structure, oh, so much to see!

She drew her attention reluctantly back to Jessie, who was saying, "This is your real home, my dear young lady. You qualify easily to remain here." Moira looked at her in surprise, "Why? What do you mean? Have I passed a test or something?"

Jessie gave her little chuckle, "Yes, my dear, you have on at least two counts. First, you are here. Remember I said that one goes to the realm most suited to their character and outlook. Any not suited by thought or action cannot enter here. Second, we know of your general helpfulness to those who needed help...."

"How do you know what I did?" Moira asked in surprise, a little embarrassed. All she had done was a little hospital visiting a few older folk. She remembered once telling Paul she was helping out a bit, and he scoffed.

"Much more than that!" Jessie continued, "Your level of consciousness is what really counts. Your awareness of self..."

"But what about Paul? How is he so different? Is that why he can't come here?"

"I'm a little afraid for Paul," Jessie stopped smiling. "He's a different case altogether. You see, he doesn't like helping anyone, and he scorns his spirituality. In time he will accept it, and there will be many opportunities given to him; if he reaches out, we can help. But he must reach. Now," she turned,

"This is your guide, Moira. She has always been near you, ready to help whenever she could, even if you knew nothing about it. Her name is Tabitha."

She turned as Jessie pointed to an approaching figure dressed in 18th-century style, a soft smile on her beautiful face, and stopped before her. As she did so, a warmth stole over Moira, a wonderful sense of belonging, of greeting a long-lost, loved companion. Peace and tranquility swept over Moira as she allowed herself to be gently embraced. Unbidden tears of pure joy blotted out her vision.

"Welcome, Moira! Welcome to your home! I'm so delighted that we can now talk together. It's awful hard to talk when you can't hear me!" Tabitha had a lovely laugh.

"But...but…" Moira stumbled, "Have I always had a guide? Why? Does everyone on Earth have a guide?" She became more articulate as she went. "I've never thought about anything like this! And why are you dressed like that?" "Like what?" was, in fact, something of the style of dress worn by early American pioneer women, long full skirts, and frilly sleeves with a bonnet. Only Tabitha had chosen colours completely foreign to the pioneer ladies. They were drab; Tabitha was not.

"Yes, it must seem strange to you," she picked up Moira's train of thought, "We were a drab lot, back in those Puritan days. Oh, we thought we were so right! We had to do some thinking when we arrived here!" She spoke with the old-world accent in keeping with her Puritan clothes. Both would have crossed the Atlantic together. Tabitha continued, "Come, let us go to my home, which I hope you will treat as your own. You can rest or talk, just as you like."

Linking arms, she led the bemused girl through a magnificent garden, along a beautiful stream, past several houses, some very large, others quite small, but everyone, without exception, fitting exactly into their surroundings. Still bemused, Moira was nevertheless delighted with the almost overwhelming beauty everywhere. They met many people as they went, friendly, cheerful people, and curiously, all about the same age. Tabitha explained. "Age is of no matter here. What usually occurs is that when someone arrives, perhaps as an elderly person, they soon adjust their new spiritual body to be as they were in their time. And usually wear what they were accustomed to. Some get different ideas and wear all kinds of dress, as you see." This brought up the differences in dress – there was everything from early Roman, Greek, Egyptian, or similar to the most modern, straight from the glossy fashion mags.

As they strolled along in the midst of such beauty, the colours, the ethereal music, Moira was more sure that she was dreaming. The tranquillity, the all-pervading peace, the beautiful people, made her afraid she might wake up.

"No, my dear Moira, this is now your world, your home. You are not dreaming. You are here; I am here; you've been to your own funeral. No, my dear, you are now at the start of your new life!"

Moira found herself gripping Tabitha's arm in an effort to gain a little reassurance on it all. So much was so surprising that she needed something to cling to. By this time, they had reached a lovely colonial cottage. Moira knew immediately that it was Tabitha's.

"Come in, dear girl. This will be your home, if you would like it. There is nothing to keep you here if you would rather go somewhere else. But I hope you would like to consider this your home. I need to go away quite a lot, so I wouldn't be in your way at all, if you would rather be alone. And I know just how you like things. You'll find it's much like your previous home. But if you don't like anything, please feel free to change whatever you like."

"Oh, no," Moira hastened to say, "This is lovely, just lovely, and…" She hesitated, afraid of being sentimental, even a little maudlin. Tabitha raised her eyebrows encouragingly.

"You're so much like the big sister I wish I had and never did!" She found it difficult to speak past the huge lump in her throat. Tabitha kissed her on the forehead, looked into her eyes, and said softly, "I am indeed just that! I have always tried to be that to you, and we have been together before; I'll tell you all about it as you become more settled here." Moira, over-come by pure joy, fell into her arms and, for perhaps the first time ever, felt perfect peace.

At that moment, life really began for her. There was much to learn, to find out - like this latest revelation, but she knew! She knew she was alive.

Paul's New Friends

"What's happened to them?" Eve growled, looking anxiously in the direction the men had gone. "Good riddance, that's what I say!" Jane sniffed. "They're nothing but trouble, that lot!"

Eve looked at her. "Maybe, maybe they are! But you remember what happened that last time they went off?" She moved restlessly about as she spoke, "Remember those two geezers who came? Remember what they did to that little girl - what was her name? If they come again, I'll kill him, that's what, and with my bare hands! But that leaves us with no-one to stand up for us". She looked at Paul and shook her head. "No, you'd be no good in a real set-to."

"How do you know?" Paul was offended. He muttered, "I might not look much to you but give me a chance! I'll show you!"

"You'll show me what?" a harsh voice belonging to a tall thin man made them spin around. "You! You won't show me anything, my fine young bucko! A pip-squeak, like you! Now, what have we here?" Brushing Paul aside with a casual sweep of his arm, he stood towering over Eve - and she was tall. "Where're your menfolk? Don't say you haven't got any! Are they far away?"

"Think I'd tell if they were," Eve growled sullenly, "They won't be long." The man stood, looking from one to the other. Finally, he grunted, "Looks like you're not worth the bother! Skinny pair of crows! And your fancy boyfriend! You keep him as a pet? God, what a miserable hole!" He turned and shambled off.

That was the first of a spasmodic stream of 'visitors' looking to see what they might take, or if not that, to beg. Paul lost no time, however, in providing them with stout poles, and giving them a little sparring practice. He knew he knew very little about such things, but he found some things seemed natural, instinctive. This proved to be a wise move, and he soon became a competent protector of both himself and his companions. Of course, he was not a bit keen on putting this to the test should Billy and his mates return. But he had to be dreaming! Otherwise, how could he now be wearing clothes - of a sort - again?

Without being aware of it, he had, in some mysterious manner, reclothed himself; not neat, not gaudy, but good enough to spare him the jibes he had received from their last assailants. There had been three of them; all bent on some unpleasantries. A few well-placed clouts had seen them off, and as they went, one of them shouted, "Ha! Like the girls, do ya! Running around naked! A bloody poof!" Paul gave chase, but respect for his cudgel sped them on their way.

It was after that when Eve tittered and pointed at him. "Look! Our boy, who is now a man, has some clothes! How did you do that? Where did you find them?" For all her derision, she had developed a respect, even a liking for him. As he looked down at his body, he saw it was indeed covered by something like a kilt. How; he hadn't the faintest idea. He thought briefly he might have wished for something to cover himself, but he had brushed that aside. He knew, didn't he? You can't just wish for something - and get it. Anyway, he thought, there were too many other strange things to ponder. He had no bruises, no stiffness, no discomfort at all. No thirst, no hunger. In spite of his not very cheerful companions and his even less cheerful surroundings, he was feeling much better than he had been. However, he felt there was something wrong. He could not quite put a finger on it. If this place is where people go when they die, he didn't think much of it. A miserable hole, as one 'visitor' put it. All these people here were a scurrilous lot, all snarling and fighting, everyone trying to outdo the other. Well, if that's the way it is, then so be it, he concluded. He had never been one for any introspection; otherwise, he might have seen himself as 'one of them,' but he did not.

"So," He looked around, "What do we do for kicks around here?" Both Eve and Jane looked at him, puzzled. "You know! Kicks, Fun, excitement!" he waved his arms about. "Oh, yeah!" Eve grinned at him, "That's a new one! Where did you learn that one? How long have you been here then if you don't know that one?" Paul snorted.

"Too bloody long!" Jane muttered savagely, "If it hadn't been for her," she glared at Eve, "I wouldn't be here now!"

"That's a lie, and you know it, you old bag!" Eve stood up angrily. "You had the gin!" "And you started the fire, you with your smoking!" "Alright! Alright! So, we're both to blame then," Eve said disgustedly, "But anyhow, it wouldn't have mattered all that much – we'd have still finished up here whenever we got it, wouldn't we?"

"That's probably right," Paul tried to restore some peace, "Are you going to tell me what happened."

"Aw, we got drunk, her and me." Jane spat, "We was havin' a good time whenever Eve 'ere got a good customer. Me, I got a bit too old, but Eve, she was a beauty, she was! Well, this night, we got drunk and set the place on fire. Next thing we know, we's both 'ere, in this bog 'ole!"

"When was that?" Paul wanted to know.

"Oh, I dunno," Jane shrugged, "King Edward was king, I think. Is 'e still king? Yes, that's right, because you remember that tart?" She looked at Eve. "Who reckoned she was one of his..."

"Yeah, and since we've been stuck in this dump," Eve groaned, "Nothing to do, nowhere to go. Some bloke came 'ere once and tried to tell us of a place he could take us - a good place, he said, 'cause we was dead, and was spirits or somethin,'" She cackled, "Spirits! The only spirits we know about is gin and God! I'd love a good swig o' gin! But it was our own doin' like, finishin' up 'ere, like this, and we got plenty of time to think about it!"

Paul could but agree, with so little to base any other course. Oh, he knew what Thomas had said, but where was the truth? Finishing up like this, as Eve said, had no real appeal. What to do? It seemed Billy and his bullies had gone. So? He took a despondent kick at a clump of dirt, and his foot struck something that drew his attention, and he thought he saw a gleam of something. He bent down and dug around with his fingers and, with a gasp of surprise, came up with a few coins. Were they gold? Maybe they were. His cry brought a quick response.

"Wot you got there?" Eve demanded, and before he could do anything, she grabbed his arm with a very strong grip he found. He opened his hand a crack and whispered, "Money! Look! Lovely money!" Four coins, heavy and golden, about twenty millimetres across, with the head of someone, and on the obverse a shield, and the figure 10,' Ten what? Eve tried to prise them from his grasp. "Give them to me! Them's ours! They been 'ere all the time, so they's ours! Come on! Give 'em to me!" Paul had no intention of obeying. With a jerk, he shook her off while Jane attacked him from the other side. He broke away again, shouting, "Stop it! Stop it! Silly old bag! Listen to me!" "I still say they's ours! Come on hand 'em over!"

"Listen to me!" Paul shouted, "Bloody-well listen, why don't you?" This brought a grudging silence. "I was about to say; I found them, and finders' keepers! But...," he held up his hand at the protest, "I'm quite prepared to share them with you because you've been good to me, so why don't you both come with me to find this tavern I went to - if we can find it, that is."

But he was very puzzled. Money in Heaven? Real money? The publican back at the inn had hinted at it, but that seemed quite normal - until he thought about it. And the more he thought, the less he understood. Money, and gold money at that? Where on Earth - no, Heaven did gold coins come from? Eve cut across his thought.

"I'll give you a good time if you give me one of those!" She said in her 'come on' voice, but Paul was not interested in the old baggage.

"No, I said I would share them, but you must come with me to get them. I promise I will not do a bunk with them - I could, you know, but I promise to share them when we find the inn. Are you coming?"

He hefted the coins enticingly in his hand, showing them at a safe distance, and he needed to say no more. Hell, anything, anything was better than hanging around this miserable hole.

"Alright then," Paul pointed - he hoped - to the right direction and took a pace, "If there's no reason why not, let's go!"

"But what about Billy and the others?" Jane asked, "He'll be mad as hell when he comes back and finds us gone!"

"I guess he would have to find us first!" Paul tried to display confidence he didn't really have, but he knew he was right.

"Let's go, then." Jane said in a loud whisper, "We don't want them coming back before we go, and since we got nothing to take with us… 'cept the money." She looked at Paul, a gleam in her eye, "How did you know there was money there? I mean…" Paul interrupted, "How could I know? You lot have been here - what, how long? Long enough, I would say. I'm just as much in the dark as you. I'd very much like to know how that money got there."

"Well," Eve said briskly, we ain't goin' to know 'anging around 'ere, so let's go!" Paul wondered about their change in attitude, but when he felt the weight of those lovely coins, he knew why.

So, they set off. But which way? Simple. If Billy had disappeared behind that rock, that was the wrong way. The opposite had to be the one. And as he looked about, he felt more and more he must have come from the way they were heading. It was a little brighter there, he was sure. And for once, he was right. They soon left the dismal glade and went for some distance, hopefully in a straight line. Paul had heard somewhere about lost people walking around in a circle. Eve, however, remarked that she thought there was more light. The change was almost imperceptible, but on a careful look, the others had to agree- it was brighter.

Several times they saw shadows that melted into the scruffy bushes, which Paul had to admit were a little less moribund than the ones where they had come from.

They were accosted only once. There were four of them, three males and one female. One shouted, "Hoy! You got any food? Or booze?" But they were unarmed, and when they saw the stout staves and determined attitude of the marchers, they backed off. Paul, feeling a little sorry, shouted, not unkindly, "No, we don't carry any." He added, "Can you tell us the way to the tavern?" The four would-be assailants shook their heads, looking blank.

For what seemed a very long time, they pressed on, meeting no-one of any note, with those they did meet standing well back. That was another thing Paul wondered about. Why were all these people they met afraid of them? None they met were of the same stamp as any of those they had brushed within the little dell with Billy and co. Was it because there were three of them? Not likely, for two were women. True, they were armed, but with no more than big sticks, which, if they were really pressed, would not count for much. There was something much more important than that, however. Paul, on glancing down and checking his footing, discovered to his utter surprise, that he was once more dressed in the smart but casual clothes he was wearing when he was killed. He looked at his trousers, jacket, and shoes, gave his head a little shake to be sure he was still awake. And as he looked at his companions, they also were no longer dressed in rags but attire of two young ladies in the fashion of the day, just a little more flamboyant than demure young ladies would wear.

Paul suddenly understood the remarks made by Jane before they left the glen. They must be London prostitutes. However, there was something incongruous in their appearance. He snorted in mirth, then could not suppress a loud guffaw. He could not stop. He literally laughed until he cried. Finally, a sharp blow on the shoulder from Jane quietened him down.

"Wot yer laughin' at, you bloody baboon?" "Wat's so bloody funny?" Paul took a deep breath as he tried to keep a straight face. At last, he was able to speak in a strangled voice. "If you two could see each other! All dressed up, strolling down Piccadilly, out in the wilderness, with these great clubs over your shoulders! You look funny here! I bet you'd look funnier if you were strolling down

Piccadilly!" A rain of blows soon quietened him down. He pleaded "Ladies! Please! Ladies! I couldn't help it – you looked so out of place!" He looked down, "So do I, I suppose."

"Yeah, well, don't you be so smart! We's got feelings too!" Jane was aggrieved.

"Yes, and I'm sorry," Paul was feeling more contrite than his usual habit, "But how do you think we got these clothes? Is that your usual style?" Both Eve and Jane looked at each other and really noticed the changes for the first time. Then Eve started to titter, and then they both started. They howled, shrieked, roared, and thumped each other, tears streaming down their faces. At last, their laughter subsided, and they clung to each other, slowly regaining their composure. At last, Eve said, "You're right, old sport! We're funny, alright! But how it happened, well, I dunno."

"All I can think of," Paul offered, "Is that we did it ourselves. Don't ask me how - but you've got what you used to wear, is that right," they both nodded. "And this is what I was wearing. So, we must have done it. But how?"

For all their amusement - tinged with a little diffidence at being seen in a near-wilderness area dressed for the city, they discovered many more they saw were dressed quite out of keeping with their surroundings. Stepped out again, feeling much better.

As they went along, all was quiet, and Paul fell to thinking about these two companions; was his original thought about them, correct? He determined to ask. Jane replied airily, "Oh, I thought you knew! We was on the Game, don't you know! We did alright, too, until I got too old. No-one wanted an old bag anymore, but Eve, she did good."

"Yeah," Eve went on, "I got some real toffs - paid real good!" They were not in the least embarrassed or reticent about their past; quite the reverse. Eve could see Paul looking slightly contemptuous and superior, so she said defensively, "How else is a poor gel to get along? We did it because there weren't nothin' else to do for a crust; at least we gave a bit o' joy to a few, and we got a bottle of gin now and then. What, do you reckon we was bad or something?"

"Oh, no!" He hastened to reassure them, "But I've never paid for it - always got it for maybe the price of a dinner, but who am I to judge? I suppose I'm no saint, so I can't criticize." So, he was in the company of two London prostitutes. On looking at them - sideways, to be not too obvious – he had to admit they were much more attractive than he thought they had been, back at the dell. Jane was now quite attractive, while Eve was definitely handsome. He also noticed that the brightness had increased considerably, and he wondered if that was the reason. He also wondered if their apparent improvement was due to being a bit short of other feminine company.

Then, at their prompting, he found himself telling them about his job with a stockbroker, his family, friends, and Moira. As he talked, he became aware of just how unpleasant he had been. He had done nothing for anyone unless there was something in it for him. And while not actually breaking any laws, he was very good at bending them as far as they would go. He recalled the time he had cooked up a little plot to borrow some money from - but unknown by - his employers to put down as a deposit on a desirable property up for sale. Fortunately, his hopes of a ready buyer were correct, and the deal went through. He made a nice little pile out of that, enabling him to return the money undetected. He didn't sleep well for a few nights after that; it had been a trifle close. He could get caught!

However, after a few more exploits (not with his employers' money - he found himself going closer to the edge by writing worthless cheques and depending heavily on luck in making a quick sale to make the cheque good, all by careful timing.

Recounting all this brought it all back to him. It was not because his companions were critical or judgemental; they laughed and joked with him. But he knew he had been sailing much too close to the wind, and very lucky to get away with it all. Further, it made him wonder what might have happened had he not met his fate that night and carried on as usual. He had a fleeting picture of himself, Scrooge-like, lots of money, and not a friend in the world.

He tried to justify his actions by saying, "Yes, but you know how it is! You've got to have money to get along, don't you? I mean, you can't do anything at all without money! If you haven't got it, geez, life's hell!"

Their talking was interrupted as they turned a bend in the path they were following. Ahead were several crude cottages, scattered about a clearing in the trees. A few people watched them approach, but they did not cower or cringe away; they stood their ground, showing neither hostility nor fear but mild interest. The whole atmosphere was different. This was a change indeed! A pleasant surprise, in fact.

They stopped a little distance from a couple standing in front of one of the cottages. Paul lowered his cudgel in what he hoped was a friendly gesture, nodded to the man, and asked, "Greetings! Can you tell us if there is a tavern somewhere around here? I went to one a little while ago, but I can't find it now."

"A little way over there!" the man said abruptly as he pointed to their right. "But you better not go there! Place was busted up by some soldiers." The man spoke in sharp phrases. "Whole place is in an uproar."

"That'll be the place," Paul answered, "And that's just what I would have thought. Was it Romans or Red Coats?" The man laughed, "Both! Seems they was shaping up for it for a long time, and the other night they got stuck into each other. Right, punch-up it was!"

"Sounds as if we'd better keep away from it. I don't want the ladies getting hurt." He looked about him at the mean-looking cottages, but he noted that they were very much better than the hovels where they came from. There was an attempt to make gardens, and there were quite a few lively-looking trees about. There was even a small stream. Why was this different from there? The whole atmosphere was an improvement, with people neither bullying nor afraid. He didn't know why.

However, they should be better off here. He decided to find out about these cottages. The idea of perhaps occupying one of them with his new friends would be good. He was actually enjoying their company, who, since the appearance of decent clothes, were laughing and joking; mostly bawdy, he noted.

He was also learning how to use the advantage of true thought transference. He knew, without any doubt, if there was any reason to distrust anyone. The couple in front of them was OK. No doubt there. Paul and the women had no hesitation in accepting an invitation into their little cottage. It was crude but clean and tidy, with a bed, a few chairs, and some curtains.

It turned out that they, too, had been killed by accident, when their yacht was wrecked on Middleton Reef, in the Tasman Sea, and they were drowned. Both Australian, they were pleased to know that Paul was from New Zealand, and they spent some time in the game of cross-Tasman rivalry and jokes.

Paul, however, wanted some hard information. How, for starters, can one get one of these cottages? Can they be bought? While not very good, they were far better than nothing, and far better than where they came from.

"No," they told him, "You can't buy them. It's a bit queer because they just seem to be here. And sometimes, one becomes empty. Why, well, we don't know why. But there's one over there on the edge of the clearing. That's empty."

It looked pretty basic to Paul, but a lot better than nothing. What if it rains? Eve wanted to know where the previous occupants had gone. She was told there was only one of them, and "He just disappeared. Some come. some go, that's all we know," they said. Some come just like you lot, they said and wondered where they had come from.

When Paul told them, the man looked surprised. "Not many ever come from there; in fact, I think you're the first I know of. Looks pretty gloomy over there. What's it like?" He laughed grimly as Paul told their tale.

"Yeah! I'm told it's a dangerous place. Bad enough here at times. A while ago, some geezer came here with some of his cronies - you know - minders, I think you call them, and said he came for the rent! We chased them off, double quick, I can tell you, and they better not come back!"

The friendly couple escorted them over to the empty cottage, which they had no hesitation in occupying when they were told that possession was the law here, so to speak, and as long as they occupied it, it was theirs. If they left - permanently – someone else could claim it for their own. They soon settled in. They had nothing other than what they stood in, so it was a simple matter of just walking in. It was furnished after a fashion, crudely, but there had been an attempt at homemaking with a few curtains and a rug or two on the floor. Paul could not identify the material of the walls or floor, not wood or any other usual material. It seemed sound enough; he pounded on the wall, and it didn't give. It was quite rigid and firm.

"Yes," he thought, "This will do until something better turns up. I wonder now if we should go and find that tavern?" The idea of holding these lovely gold pieces in his hand was exciting; that would restore his confidence!

Moira's Education Begins

Moira flopped into a chair and let out a huge sigh. She had just returned with Tabitha after a tour of their immediate surroundings. "Oh, what a wonderful place! I know you say it isn't Heaven, but it must be something like it."

"No," Tabitha pointed out, "But remember, this is only one of many realms. This is the place where those who have lived caring, helpful lives are most likely to come to," she chuckled. "And they are often surprised when they discover that their religious background is of little consequence unless, of course, they followed and used - the teachings of the Master Jesus. Those that merely went to church on Sundays often do not come here!" Tabitha shrugged. "We'll talk more about that another time. Tell me, what has attracted your interest the most?"

Moira sat collecting her thoughts. There was so much she had seen. "I think," she started slowly, "The first thing is the peace, the tranquillity. Oh, and it's all so beautiful!" The words came faster now, "The gardens and trees! And that fruit! I've never tasted anything like it. Oh, and the houses! They just fit in so perfectly!"

She was to spend some little time contemplating and savouring all she had seen. Tabitha had taken her to a children's creche. There, she saw children from many places, some from accidents, abortions, and miscarriages, but they were mainly from North African countries and India, such places where their children had no great value and less of a future. They came here to the realm where children were treated as treasures.

Overwhelmed by the sight of these shreds of humanity arriving in a steady stream, she turned away, unable to watch. But Tabitha knew how to remedy that. She led the way a short distance to where these pitiful victims of greed, ignorance, and brutality were recovering. Here, she saw the tender, loving care lavished on these mites. These who should inherit the Earth. Here, there was laughter and joy. For them, this was indeed Heaven.

The smiles, the hope, and the love shining from their eyes were too much for her. Leaning on Tabitha, she buried her face in her hands, aghast at the outrage committed against these defenceless ones, and she was determined to be one of those who were, at last, giving these children the love and care needed so desperately.

Then she was taken to the Concert Bowl. This was adjacent to the children's centre and was difficult to miss. Some called it the Music Bowl, and others called it the Beethoven Basin, for it was he, reputedly, who was the originator of the idea.

It was just that; a huge bowl, tiers upon tiers of seats soaring upwards, sinking down to the centre, wherein was the stage. There was to be a performance in a short time, and while Moira had not been a musician, she had a fair appreciation of that art, although her knowledge of the Mozart/Hayden/Bach/Beethoven genre was sketchy.

Tabitha pressed her to stay, for she said it would be an experience not to be missed. So they sat and observed the phenomenon of the enormous bowl filling in an unusual way. People just suddenly appeared before her.

"How do they do that?" she asked in a hushed voice. "Oh, you'll get used to that!" Tabitha said airily, "People do that all the time here! We can be anywhere we want, here, as you will soon find out."

"You mean...people teleport themselves?" Moira was fast reaching the point of not being surprised anymore. "I don't know what that means," Tabitha answered with a little frown, "But it's quite normal. And as you have seen, we can fly when we want to, just as easily." Further questions would have to wait, for the stage was fast filling with musicians, arranging themselves in traditional orchestral form, and began their customary tuning of instruments. A hum of anticipation coming from all sides suddenly stopped as the conductor emerged, bowed to the huge audience, and turned to the orchestra.

It was not until after the concert that Moira suddenly became aware that, although they were sitting about halfway up this gigantic bowl, her view of the stage was as from a few feet away! And the conductor was also as close as that.

Further, his face was somehow familiar to her. She had seen it before somewhere, and after this, her first memorable concert in the higher realms, she was to make a point of attending subsequent performances. Although her musical education was rudimentary, she could recognise – when the music reached that point - that this was Beethoven's Ninth Symphony, the Choral, and that it was he who was conducting.

The 'Ode to Joy' was sung by an invisible choir, surrounding and pervading the whole universe, it seemed.

The power, beauty, and joy were reflected, first, in the conductor's face. For now, he was hearing his wonderful music and in the reception by the audience, who were literally in ecstasy.

Moira had never, in her wildest imaginings, ever thought that music could be so powerful, so moving. She sat, utterly enthralled.

And that was not all. It was not until later that she remembered the colours. The entire area above the concert bowl was alive with colour, which pulsed, throbbed, formed, and dissolved in keeping with the music. This was to become an important way to prepare for higher learning. It was a very uplifting experience. Concerts were given regularly by any one of several famous musicians, who often performed one of their well-loved works.

It didn't stop there, either. Many of the Old School were finding new ways to express their ideas. Mozart was a favourite at this because of the wonderful colour symphonies he was always producing.

And it was not only the 'classical' musicians. There were quite a few moderns, such as one might hear on a 'pop' radio programme, but minus the raucous din in vogue on the Earth-plane. Further, there was a huge supply of very able orchestral musicians of all types; with their standards so high, their understanding and rapport with their conductor made every performance a golden gem not to be missed.

However, Moira was not so taken by all this nor so thoughtless as to believe that this was all there was to live here. And she had never fallen for the golden streets, endless harp playing of heavenly choirs, forever standing before the Throne of God praising Him and His works. She could not imagine anything more soul-destroying than that. So, what did people do?

"That's just where I'm taking you, young lady! Come on, and you'll see how we keep busy."

And as suddenly they were flying. No vertigo, no fear, no discomfort. Just up and away. Tabitha had her arm around Moira's shoulders, and off they went, soaring effortlessly over the beautiful land. There were lakes, streams, and buildings, large and small, melding into their surroundings perfectly.

"Who looks after all this? And who designed it?" Moira's eyes were everywhere in an effort to take it all in.

"There are specialists in every vocation you can think of, and probably many you can't!" Tabitha gave her little laugh, "All these experts worked in these crafts before coming here, and many are delighted to be able to carry on doing the same. I have a good idea of what you will want to do, but you should just settle in for a little while first. That is why we are just looking. When you want to - if you want to," she corrected, "You can go to any of the Universities. There's one over there!" She pointed to a beautifully proportioned, very large building, with domes, turrets, towers, and huge halls. "There, you can learn the true history of Earth, and you will find it rather different from what you might have been taught. You will enjoy the library here too. There are many more than just one, as well. This one serves just this area, and you will find every book, ancient or modern, ever written on Earth, and of course, that means all those lost to modern scholars on Earth." That was only the start. Tabitha was kept very busy trying to answer the barrage of questions. She pointed out the music centre, the numerous lecture halls, and even the science laboratories, a further surprise.

And, of course, the many hospitals. This raised Moira's eyebrows. "Why do you need hospitals? Do people have accidents here, then?"

"Oh, no, never! Not here! But, of course, this is still all new to you." Tabitha had a wonderful knack for being amused without being superior or condescending. "We need them here because there are so many arrivals who know absolutely nothing about themselves or where they are likely to go when their Earth-life is done. You know only too well how most people fear death, and just as many believe that when they die, that's the end of everything. Total - how do you say it? - Wipe-out. Even the religious ones are afraid of death. I often think so much for their faith!"

"These are places of rest and adjustment for those who come to us here after long, painful illnesses where there is often much suffering. They often arrive as they departed from the physical, in a coma, and they need to recover as smoothly as we can arrange. Often husbands and wives already here will be present when the new one revives. And as you will know, there are many who come to us like that. Thus, we need all these rest homes.

"If they only knew," she shrugged sadly, "That the transition is a very easy and painless thing to do - as easy as walking through a door."

"Yes, I know now." Moira answered, "I know how easy it is, but before that, I was afraid, like most others."

"One usually learns about this when it's too late to be of any real use to them." Tabitha made a little grimace.

"But how can they learn about any of this before they die?" Moira indicated the scene below, "Who knows about death and dying? It's useless asking them because even the priests and ministers don't know. None of them talk about anything like this! How can they find out?"

"It's easy enough for those who really want to find out," Tabitha answered after a moment, "But there are several obstacles on the Earth-plane. The society I was in, and much the same for yours, does not encourage questions like that, especially the churches. Our church said we would be working with the devil if we started asking such questions, for they said we were questioning our faith if we did."

"Then, more in your time, the experts in the universities all went around saying that we came from a sea of slime, and we would return there; you know how they say it - Man is an Animal, a clever one at that, but an animal, and when he dies, there is nothing, because there is nothing that can survive. If you go to the University here, you will learn how they came to that conclusion. I am only a simple woman and don't understand those things."

"But I said that if anyone wanted to learn, we have been working to help them for many years. You know of one of the most important teachers who went to the Earth-plane to do just that." She could see the understanding in Moira's eyes, "Yes, that's right. It was Jesus of Nazareth. You will learn the entire truth about Him and His ministry in due course."

"And many more have since then managed to burst through the fog of ignorance on Earth. In recent times there have been several important penetrations, and now quite a few are teaching and providing channels and links to allow us to work through and teach many more."

"Oh?" Moira was puzzled, "Who are they? I haven't heard of anyone like that, unless you mean these so-called mediums, these spiritualists. They are all frauds, aren't they?"

"Alas, there were many frauds, misleading people. But for every bad one, there are many genuine ones, who work closely with us. They heal many who come to them, they teach many more, and show many more that there is no death, but survival, and a very full life."

As she finished speaking, she steered Moira towards a lovely open park, dotted with lovely trees, small lakes, and a few buildings grouped at one end.

"But we rush ahead too fast. You will learn all of that later. Just now we're sightseeing. And so, sights we shall see." She pointed ahead.

"There, in that park, is one of our animal refuges." She glanced out of the corner of her eyes to see the reaction to that. She grinned inwardly as Moira, as expected, looked surprised. "Animal refuge? I didn't know…"

"Of course, you didn't! But let me assure you that it's true. That's another thing Earth folk are ignorant about. Animals are much the same as us. Oh, don't get me wrong. That doesn't mean we are on their level. No, it means that they, as well as us, are creatures of God and, as such, are spiritual."

"Wild animals are not at the same level as domestic ones who have been in contact with us for a long time. Here, you will find many cats, dogs, horses, and all those that have been family pets. As you know, many become very attached, both ways. And as they often pass to this world before their beloved humans, they are cared for until their masters show up. We see many joyful and unexpected reunions in this park!"

"Do you think…" Moira's eyes shone in anticipation, "I would find my two Siamese cats?" she asked hopefully. "I'll be very surprised if you don't!" Tabitha laughed, "Come on, let's find them."

They started down slowly, for Tabitha thought it best to prepare her. She knew Moira had been very fond of her cats and had even written a few lines when the last of the pair left the Earth-plane. She asked, "What about that little thing you wrote?"

"How did you know about that?" Moira was embarrassed. "How did you …" "Sh...I know many things about you, remember! I was your guide. Say it for me, won't you? Please?"

When Moira first tried to read what she had written, she found she could not. Even now, she found it hard. But Tabitha encouraged her. She cleared her throat.

"I called it 'To Sheba' because I had her longer than her sister. I loved them both very much." In a voice she found hard to control, she started….

How do you say goodbye?
How do you farewell a friend who has come to your call
Who has warmed your bed
Who has looked to you for sustenance and care
Who, with her demanding voice
Her prodigious leaps
Her insistence on sharing your food
Has invaded your life?
Who, with a clever calculated leap, would reduce the avian population by one
Who would sit with feline patience waiting at the gate
Who, with her big round eyes, would stare her way right into your very soul?
How do you say goodbye to one so loved as she
Whose Earthly life has run its course
To leave us so desolate?
Perchance, in the bright Elysian Fields
A slender Seal-point Siamese will come again
In answer to her name, as she has done un-numbered times
On this, the Earth-bound plane."

"You must have loved her very much," Tabitha said softly, "I am looking forward to meeting them!" Moira paused – "Oh, do you think so, but how are we going to find them? It's huge down there?"

Tabitha laughed, "Not difficult, my dear! Remember the end of your poem? Well, here are the bright Elysian Fields you spoke of. By the way, whatever made you think of that? You were quite right, weren't you? So, call them!"

To Moira's utter astonishment and delight, two dark streaks bore down on them. She barely had time to extend her arms to them as they leapt, landing one on each arm. To overcome for speech, she cradled the two ecstatic cats, both vying for her attention. With tears streaming down her face, she proudly showed Tabitha her two beautiful cats. It was some time before she was able to speak, and then only in a strangled whisper.

"This is Sheba," she held her forward, "And her sister, half-sister really, is Laani" Both cats smirked, purring deeply, nudging Moira and looking up at Tabitha.

"That's us, and we know we're beautiful! And we are very glad our beloved human has come to us at last!"

"But...But..." Moira spluttered, "You spoke! You spoke! I can't believe it!" Sheba contented herself by looking smug, rubbing her head on Moira's arm.

"Oh, yes, they give us their thoughts!" Tabitha nodded at the cats, "Now, who is the most beautiful?" Immediately came the response, "I am!" from both. This started a dialogue between cats and humans in which Moira joined, all the while certain she was dreaming. Then a white rabbit ran past, and she found she was quite disappointed because it was not muttering, "I'm late! Oh, my ears and whiskers!"

However, it was all too much for her, and she sank down on the grass, on the hillside overlooking the lovely tranquil scene. Before long, still fondling her cats, she slowly stretched out and drifted off into a deep, dreamless sleep.

Paul's Journey

The moment their Australian friends left, Eve pounced on Paul. "Have you still got that money? Remember, you promised us some if we found the tavern!"

"Yes, I did, but we're not there yet. And yes, of course, I've still got them. And" to forestall her next question, "You can't see them, either."

"Then how do I know you still got 'em?" She was suspicious. "Of course, I've still got them," he answered sharply, "and you still can't see them!"

Eve, still suspicious, glowered at him.

"I said I'd share with you, and I will, when we find the tavern. So why don't we go?" He thought he might be better off on his own, but he found he had a twinge of something completely foreign to his nature; he found he had a thought for the two old hookers. He felt they needed a bit of a break, so he would not desert them with his little fortune. He knew it was not very much, but when you're skint, well, anything is a fortune!

"Come on," he urged, "We've come a long way for this." Eve, the more particular of the two, wanted to fuss with her dress, hair, and general appearance, and went about trying to find a mirror, muttering because she couldn't find one. She pointed at the wall beside the bed and growled, "There should be one right there!"

They all froze in disbelief. Right where she was pointing, was a mirror! Shocked, they stared in awe, almost. But the impact was quickly lost on Eve, who wailed, "Oh, Gawd! Wot a bloody awful sight! I got to do somethin'. I look terrible!" She tried unsuccessfully to preen herself, and it was not until Jane came to her rescue that she calmed down.

In fact, if she but realised it, she had shed years of wrinkles and sagging jowls and was now a striking figure, complete with an ostrich-plumed hat and a feather boa.

Paul watched, dazed by the turn of things, becoming more confused by the minute. Mirrors just don't appear, or old hags become next to youthful. He wondered what was about to happen next. His attention was torn from Eve to Jane, the transformation from the old woman to beautiful was complete.

The others then persuaded him to look himself over, and even as he watched, his reflected image changed from seedy office clerk to handsome young executive. He was later to learn how unimportant such little trifles as a cultivated image was. He would one day realise what a facade such things were. But right now, it was important to look right. And he thought they all looked just right.

He gathered his charges and herded them out the door. "This way, I think." He pointed along the path indicated by their Australian friends, "This is the way they said!"

And it was actually a very short walk. They had barely left the cottage, gone maybe two hundred metres, and they could see it through the trees. It seemed a much busier place than on his last visit, with people coming and going along several paths. And it seemed bigger. Had he been away long enough for it to be enlarged? Surely not. But, of course, he had no way of knowing. This business of no night or day, no clocks, was very inconvenient. Paul was starting to be more than a little dubious about this Heaven stuff.

Nothing, not one single thing, seemed to be what anyone might expect. What the Hell - he shrugged it all off and urged his two 'girls' in through the entrance. There, things had changed to what they had been. Gone were the Roman soldiers and Red Coats. The long bar was still there, but now there were pleasant seats and tables - still crude - to his yuppie fastidious mind, but a considerable improvement to what had been before. The atmosphere was also more respectable, with a scattering of women as well as men. This time he breasted the bar with confidence.

"Oh, it's you again, is it? You got money this time?" The barman was just as gruff as before. Paul slapped a coin down. "Will this do?" He demanded.

'Watch it! Don't get smart with me," the man growled, "I eat your kind for breakfast! Alright, let's get a look at it." He picked it up, bounced it, bit it, turned it over a couple of times, and shrugged, "Yeah, I guess it's OK. What'll you have?"

"I'll have a gin, a double, and a bit o' lemon!" Eve said archly.

"You on the Game, sister? If you are, you got plenty of competition! We got plenty of your sort round here!" He poured the drinks as he spoke, "Never seen so many tarts in one place," he grumbled, "All hanging around looking for customers, or someone to buy them drinks. Where you from, sister? Ain't seen you or your friend before." He nodded towards Jane.

"Oh, over the way a bit. And wot's wrong with the trade? A gel's got to make a living somehow!" Eve replied.

The barman grunted and went off to serve someone else. Paul picked up the drinks, two gins and a whiskey and nodded towards an empty table. The girls sat on either side of Paul almost as if to protect him or just to be closer to him – he was not sure. After a sip at his drink, he spread the coins out before him and meticulously divided them into three even piles. The girls accepted them, snatching them up with great smiles. Jane squeezed his arm in thanks, "We knew you wouldn't cheat us! You're a good feller!" He was more pleased than he ever thought he would be; he had, for maybe the first time, done something for someone else, and he found it was far less painful than he had thought.

They were in the middle of examining the coins, trying to work out their value, when there was a clatter from outside, heralding the entry of two men dressed in early American style: buckskins and coon-skin hats.

"Hoy there, Frankie!" the first man bellowed. He was not only tall, he was massive. Grinning hugely, he strode across the room, threw a bag of something that jingled down on the bar, and shouted, "The drinks are on me! Come on, name your poison, Everyone!" The man radiated power. He must have been someone back on Earth and had managed to establish himself here. He was no Billy the Bruiser, however, for there was no fear or dislike showing in any of the bar's customers, who flocked up for their drinks.

Paul tried to be unaffected by the man; he sat rolling his glass in his hand. Casually, he quaffed his drink - very good too, he noted - and as if by magic, a man appeared with a full one. The barman must have a good organisation, he thought. He leaned over and quietly asked Eve, "Do you know who he is? Seems like a pretty big cheese!"

"I dunno, but he looks alright, don't he? I wouldn't like to be his enemy, though!"

The man turned to them and said affably, "You're new here, I think. That right?" Paul nodded. The man went on, "I don't get to come here as much as I like, and it's good to meet new folk. Do you mind if I set here a spell?" Taking it for granted, he dragged a chair out and sat between Paul and Eve. He spoke again.

"Since you're new here, you don't know who I am. I got me self a spread over the hills a ways, got a nice big house, plenty good fightin' men to keep the spooks away" He laughed heartily, "Jest a joke, really! Ain't no spooks hereabouts! You gotta go 'way over the other way. Then you'll find 'em. But I like to keep a good little ole army, you know, just to keep everythin' nice and tidy" He took a good swig at his glass and shouted for a refill, "And another for my new friends here!" He turned back to them.

"My name's Crockett, Davy Crockett. Maybe you've heard of me? Used to be a senator, back in the good ole days. What's your name?"

Paul told him their names, and he couldn't keep the thought hidden about the old song; Davy Crockett, killed himself a bear when he was only three. Crockett laughed, "No, that's all hokum! I ain't killed no bear when I wus only three!"

He ordered more drinks to be brought, and Paul noticed a general increase in the noise level as the patrons made steady inroads into Crockett's money. Paul was also feeling the effect of several neat shots of whiskey. He wondered at that but was not in a very good state to pursue it. If he were supposed to be a spiritual being, how come whiskey could make him drunk? He found out how and why, but not until very much later. Just now, he tried to grasp what Crockett was telling him.

"Yes, I got me quite a spread over the hills a ways. What do you do? Are you a blacksmith? No, you're too cityfied for that. Or are you a tin-horn gambler? No, that's not you, either. So, what are you?"

Paul replied, "I'm an accountant. Or I was, before I landed up here!"

"Hm. Accountant, eh? Can't say, as I've got much use for -- one of those. I need good strong men who don't mind a good ol' scrap."

Paul wondered how it was that, in this, the land of the dead, everyone acted as though they were alive! Hotels, hookers, fighting men; all this is just like home. Even the booze tastes real. "Now, this character acts as if he owns the joint! Davey Crockett, eh? I wonder where Jim Bowie is then?"

"Or am I dreaming, about to wake up at any time?" All this rushed through his mind as he sat looking at his glass. Then, belatedly, he wondered how much of that was being picked up by Crockett, but he needn't have worried; Crockett was shouting across the room to someone at the bar.

Of all the things Paul had seen and done since his transition from Earth, he could only wonder how in Heaven, or whatever - did all of this remain totally unknown back there. Surely, someone, somewhere, must know about it. They did know, but Paul had never been in a position to find out. The situation was normal for Planet Earth. All anyone ever said was, when you die, you go to Heaven - that is, if you're good. Or they said just the opposite. You only live once, so make the best of it, because then you're dead. Dead, and that's it. Nothing else after that. Finish. And none of them seemed to be right! And not for the first time, he questioned his action of leaving the first contact point he had had with Jessie and Thomas. At least, they were able to answer some of his queries. Not like here; nobody knows anything. He might just as well be back with his BMW, and affluent lifestyle, although he realised it was his own doing to have come here.

He reluctantly decided he must accept his lot, and on looking around at the other patrons in the bar, he shrugged in acceptance. In some ways, it could be good fun; no cops to bother you, plenty of girls by the look of it, and no chance of VD, AIDS, or such. "But hang on! Steady down!" he admonished himself sharply, "I don't know that! So, I'd better not be too hasty. This place looks so much like home; it could very well be the same, even to that!"

He wondered how Moira was getting on and whether she missed him. Suddenly he saw her, as clearly as if she were beside him. He jerked upright in surprise.

"Hullo Paul!" She gave a little smile, although she was not over-pleased to see him, "Still at the drink, I see!" Paul tried to ignore the barb, "Oh, Moira, it's nice to see you. How are you, and what are you doing these days?"

"I'm going to University just now," she answered a trifle archly. "I see by your companions you are your usual self!"

He felt a little miffed by her attitude but was determined to keep his cool. "University? Where are you then? There's nothing like that around these parts! Can I come and see you?"

"No, Paul, you cannot. I've been told to tell you, that you must stay here until you are ready. Then you will be able to come. If you can make it, I'll be pleased to see you. Now I must go; there's a lecture I don't want to miss. Goodbye!"

He could not prevent fingers from running up his spine at the magic of seeing her just by thinking of her; no, not just seeing her - she was there, in front of him. Even the best technology on Earth was just getting around to vision-phones.

His attention was brought back to the here and now – if that's what it was - by Davy Crockett towering over him. "Well, boy, it seems I can use you, out at the ranch if you want to come. If you don't, never mind, you might want to someday. It's just over the hill; you can't miss it" He turned away to talk to some others beside him, leaving Paul in a quandary. Talking to Moira had unsettled him.

If there were universities, what else would there be? She said he could not go there, that he wasn't ready. What in Hell did that mean? Not ready? In what way? He had to admit he hadn't the faintest idea. But he knew what he would do. Abruptly he decided to go and find her. Who were they to tell him he wasn't ready?

He turned to Eve beside him. "You go with Davy. And maybe Jane would like to go too. Looks like a good place to go. I want to do something else. I might come and see you sometime." He tapped Crockett on the shoulder, and said, as the man turned, "Thanks for the offer, but I have something I have to do?"

"Don't be such a fool, ducky!" Eve remonstrated, "He looks alright to me, and he'll treat us good, you see, and it should be good fun. So why don't you come along?"

But Paul was resolute. "Did you see that girl who was here a few minutes ago?" Eve nodded, "Yeah, who was she? Looked a real toffee-nose."

"I was going to marry her. I want to go and find her." Eve scoffed.

"Fiddle-faddle! I can give you a better time that she can! Proper little prude, I'll bet!"

"No, she's not," defended Paul, "She's just been brought up..."
"Go and find her then! Huh! I thought you was a bright boy! Huh" Her scorn was all he needed. As casually as he could, he stood up, nodded to her, and without a backward glance, sauntered to the door.

Outside, he paused a moment, trying to analyse his behaviour. This was not him. Not like him at all, turning down what might be a good chance of a good living to go off on a fool's quest, like some damn-fool knight going into who knows what peril, just on a whim. But he knew why he had made the decision. For all his stupidity, and his selfish, cavalier attitude, he still loved Moira, and in all the mystery and turmoil of this strange but strangely familiar place, he missed her deeply.

So, he had to go and try to find her, come what may. And in this unpredictable place, what may come?

Moira Settling In

An indeterminate time later, Moira awoke from a deep, restful sleep to find her beloved Laani lying in the crook of her arm, four legs in the air, sound asleep. This had been one of her favourite positions. She looked fondly at the cat.

"Just as you always did! You beautiful thing, you haven't changed at all." Laani stirred, opened her eyes, and looked straight into Moira's.

"Took you long enough to get here! Me and Sheba have been waiting for ages!" Astonishingly clear and lucid, her thoughts came across. Moira had gone past, remarking on the wonderful things that were happening around her, and it was a sheer delight to talk to the cats. Sheba had joined them, and the beautiful seal-point Siamese cats solemnly stared as only cats can stare.

"Oh, I missed you two terribly!" She hugged both cats, "And I love you both very much."

"Oh, you've found your loved ones!" The voice belonged to a lady dressed in English country tweeds, very much an English lady, with a gentle manner and friendly face. However, it was not her dress, her manner, or her voice that made Moira sit up in surprise. There was a gorgeous lioness beside the lady, whose hand was caressing her ears. The lioness rubbed her huge head against her thigh in sheer pleasure, then she stretched languidly, lay down with that great head inches from Moira, who was certain she said "Hullo" and looked calmly into her eyes. She tried to inch away from those massive fangs. Did she actually speak?

The lady laughed. "Stroke her head. She loves that, don't you, Elsa?" as she sat beside Moira. "My name's Joy. What's yours?" Then it all fell into place. She was sitting next to a very famous lady, who had written books about her experiences with this lioness named Elsa. There had even been a film. Joy Adamson gave a little laugh.

"Yes, that's right, and it all seems so long ago now. But I'm really lucky; I have the entire pride with me now, and we are one big family. I have the big cats and you, the little beauties here." The two Siamese looked with bored nonchalance at their big cousin, not in the least disturbed by her. "So, tell me about yourself, and these two lovelies!"

The tale was soon told, how she had acquired them. They had a rather unusual relationship. They both had the same sire, but Sheba, the younger, was also the aunt of the other, Laani, so they were doubly related.

This was all quickly told, and Moira followed with a barrage of questions, to which Joy held up her hands. "Hang on! Hang on!" She laughed, "Let's have them one at a time!" Moira grinned apologetically and took a deep breath, "Well, how do animals come here when they die? Are they spirit beings just like us?"

"Most definitely they are! That's how your lovely cats, and mine, and many, many more, of all types, come here to wait for their human friends. This is true for those with close contact with humans. Those with little or no contact, such as the truly wild ones, seem to belong to what's best described as a group soul. These ones, here, being close to us, are more developed than the wild ones, just as we, in contact with those higher than us, are more developed. And so, your cats – and my lions - can communicate with us."

"So, it really was Laani who asked me why I was so long in

coming here?" "Indeed," Joy smiled as Moira leaned forward eagerly. "It was. You got the concept, not the words, of course, although it seems like it."

"With all 'this' then," Moira hesitated, "It's quite wrong for us to kill animals, even for food?" "That's a curly one, my girl! It isn't easy to answer. It's very wrong to hunt for sport, just for a trophy, a tiger skin, or elephant tusks. What we must learn is that life, and I mean all life, including our humble selves, is created by the Infinite Spirit. All life, be it trees, animals, birds, all life. No exceptions."

"And when the Almighty gave us humans dominion over all these things, he did not give us the licence to plunder, exploit or destroy any of His creatures, or even Mother Earth herself, also a living entity."

"You know only too well," Joy continued, "How Humanity has ravaged his world, now very nearly reached the point of no return. All because 'man' is completely ignorant about himself, and his status. So, dear girl, be grateful, after all, that we have dished out to them, that these lovely creatures still come to us in trust and love!"

As Joy spoke, a picture of a gentle society unfolded, where Man and Nature lived in true harmony, a world longed for by the truly sentient children of the Great Spirit. That, and much more, passed between them as they sat, surrounded by loved and loving animals. Moira could only wonder, if Joy Adamson was right, at the cause of the appalling reversal of thinking, outlook, and behaviour from the Beginning - the 'Creation,' when Mankind was made in God's image. She was to find the answer before much longer. She was told about the true road to salvation, to life everlasting, and that she was taking the first faltering steps along that road. There were many dedicated souls ready and willing to help and guide.

She was taught the difference between information and knowledge, and how to convert information to knowledge, that being immeasurably senior. She was given a glimpse into the vastness of the Spirit realms, and how one may go easily to a lower realm, but how one must earn the entrance to a higher realm.

She was told that the realm they were in was usually the highest attainable by most ordinary folk. To go directly to a higher realm was not at all common, even for those who believed they should be at the right-hand of God. This was very interesting, for it meant that most so-called highly religious leaders, 'Princes' of the Church, and so on, were in for a huge surprise on arrival. No Pearly gates, no streets of gold. No Cherubim or Seraphim, no heavenly choirs or harpists.

"Oh, yes, the golden streets are there along with those immeasurably more advanced, more senior, and therefore much more 'spiritual' than us." Joy said with a little wry grin, "We still need these bodies to function; they do not. No doubt you will see one of these masters before long, and you will know what I mean."

"You mean, someone like Jesus? Was he real?" "Yes indeed, he was real," Joy laughed, "And you will learn a great deal about Him as you progress." She stood up as she spoke, "Those high levels are not for us; we have a long way to go before we take even one step upwards!"

"Now, I must be off. I have many charges in my little park, and they need me and my helpers. It has been nice meeting you, oh, and your cats, of course, and please come and see me sometime. Just over the park."

As she and her lioness sauntered off, Moira sat a little bemused by it all. There was a great deal to digest, but as Joy pointed out, data must become knowledge before it would be of value. And that was done only one way. Experience.

She sat, savouring the scene before her. There were several people in sight, most of them with animals, many dogs, cats, of course, a few horses, and not a few birds.

Not for the first time, she wondered when she would wake up. The entire atmosphere, the ambience was so tranquil and secure in some manner, she could not define. Everyone she met was relaxed and friendly without being effusive or possessive, just a calm acceptance of one for another. And they were not glum or morose. There was a sparkle in their eyes, a merriment not far below the surface, ready to burst out at the slightest encouragement.

However, this was not to say they were flippant. A warm regard and respect for others brought a feeling of trust and dependency, never before experienced. This was repeated again and again when she started to attend classes at the University which was within easy strolling distance from the cottage.

She arrived expecting to be very much the 'new girl,' but this was not so. She was welcomed and made instantly at home. A lady introduced her to the curriculum, which was very loose. There was a series of lectures on all subjects that anyone could wish for at any level of progress. All she had to do was find on the schedule, the subjects she wanted, and all lessons were there, tabulated and updated constantly.

The entire establishment was humming with activity, with people of all ages coming and going, laughing, and singing. During lessons or lectures, however, one could have heard the proverbial pin drop.

She quickly became absorbed in a study of Earth's history and was constantly amazed at how far from the truth most historians had strayed. Interspersed with history, she became very interested in people. This was awakened by one lecture she attended.

The Lecturer said, "Humankind is almost a dual personality. There is the higher self, and the lower self. The higher is honourable, honest, considerate, and understanding of others. The lower self is what, the higher is not. It is goodness reversed. It is mean, promises health, wealth, and happiness, but robs rather than gives. Any gift is more likely rotten apples, and things leading to wretchedness."

"The earthly lives of humanity are lived, in part, for the purpose of allowing the higher self the opportunity of gaining ascendency over the lower, carnal self. If that is done, one can expect to have earned their transition to this realm."

"Those who live so as to nourish their lower selves must go to the realms more suited to their carnal tastes and propensities. As you folk are here, you have made a good start in your upward progress. You all have developed, fully or in part, the attributes of your higher selves, the part of you closest to the Infinite Spirit. Along with humility, you have a grace of spirit, an innate understanding of your companions, and a willingness to help one another beyond the thought of recompense."

The Lion Lady possessed these qualities, and Moira was to learn just how her past views and actions towards others had brought her to this happy state, and why Paul had some distance to go before he could expect to join her. She was not sure she wanted that, particularly when she caught his thought about her.

A trifle nonplussed, she was not sure what she should do. Tabitha, who had been busy elsewhere, came to the rescue as she sensed her uncertainty.

"Go to him, Moira, and I'll watch you from here. You will come to no harm, and it could possibly help him."

So, she went. Just by picturing him, she went. She looked with distaste at the crude room, the uncouth-looking people, and the drabness. She barely suppressed a shudder at the sight. It was not that she was a prude. After all, she had become engaged to the one she now saw before her, although, as she looked, she wondered why.

She had to confess to enjoying herself, but that did not mean acting rudely or crudely. And drinking to insensibility was a foolish thing to do. She had to confess that the probable reason for accepting his proposal was his affluence. And she also believed that when they were married, she would be able to wean him off the bottle.

Her distaste at seeing him in a bar was involuntary. He looked nothing like the sartorial young man she knew. Disappointed in him - as she had a genuine liking for him - she decided to leave and was surprised at the abruptness of her return to Tabitha. It only took a blink, and she was again in the pleasant cottage she had been invited to call home. A huge sigh escaped her as she sat, the two cats immediately occupying her lap.

"Oh......What a terrible place! It's so drab and crude. And the people I saw looked no better. Just...Agh!"

"Agh is right, in comparison to our plane here. You understand you have just visited the next lower plane? The one often called the Astral Plane?" Moira nodded, "Yes, but why is it that they don't want to learn about themselves? They seem intelligent enough; Paul is - or was - quite bright…"

"They are nowhere near ready to come here. Remember what you told me the lecturer said? About their lower selves? Well, until they start reaching, nothing much will happen. A few are beginning to open their spiritual eyes and to ask the right kind of question." Tabitha came over, sat beside her, and continued, "Nobody is ready to learn anything until they start reaching, and that happens when they discover they don't know. Then they want to know, even demand it. Then we can step in and help. But something usually triggers this off. It sometimes happens that someone will hold out a genuinely warm helping hand without expecting a reward of some sort. This alone raises their spiritual awareness even when they don't see this happening, and this puts them directly in a receptive state, and often, in a short time, they can then accept a transition to this realm, and then they can really start learning."

Tabitha continued. "Also, I'm quite sure you have realised by now that Service is the oil that lubricates the wheels of these realms. One 'pays one's way,' so to speak, by service to others. Now, that's quite enough of my lecturing. All this will be taught as you continue at school."

Paul and Jane

Jane looked up in surprise as Paul entered the little cottage alone.

"Ullo! Wot you done wif 'er?" She glared suspiciously at him.

'Oh, she'll be along very soon; in fact, here she comes!" He pointed down the path. There, a small convoy appeared led by Davy Crockett with Eve at his side. He seemed to be quite taken with her.

"Ho, my lad, you got here first! Well, what about our friend here? Eve's been tellin' me all about her. Have you told her where we're off to?" Paul shook his head. "No, I've just got here ahead of you, and there's been no time." Eve quickly told Jane all about it, who, reluctant at first, became more so as Eve finished saying, "So I'm going along, and you're coming too. He (nodding at Davy) says it's alright."

"No, I like it here! We got this lovely little 'ouse, and it suits me fine! 'Sides, I've had enough traipsin' around. I just want to stay put for a while. You go and enjoy yourself! I'll see you sometime." She turned away as she finished and curled up in her chair like an old woman.

Eve looked at her for a moment, and gave a little shrug. "Yeah, well I s'pose you know best, and I can't make you." She looked at Davy, who also shrugged. "Well, I'll be seein' you then. Now take care, you see! Oh!" She turned back to Jane, "Davy tells me there's plenty more where these came from." She dropped several gold coins into Jane's lap, "You'll have a use for them, over at the tavern." She turned to Paul, "How about you? Are you coming with us? Or are you still going to look for that fancy piece? Don't forget I can give you a much better time than she can!" Paul stood undecided for a moment, but a tiny corner of Moira's world had been lifted. It had become very desirable, an El Dorado, a Shangri La; a quest that must be pursued, come what may.

Davy Crockett patted him paternally on the shoulder, "OK, lad, we understand. You go on your search and good luck. If you ever pass my way, we'll be pleased to have you." He turned and bawled, "Come on, you lot! Let's get on the road! Come on, you lazy good-for-nothin's! Move!"

Eve stood in indecision for a moment. Only for a moment, though; the lure of money was too much to resist. "Ta ta then!" She said with an embarrassed sniff, turned, and followed Crockett. "What are you going to do?" Jane asked Paul, "Or would you like to stay with me? I'd be all alone if you go. An old lady needs someone."

"Oh, I'm not staying, although I must say I was tempted to go with them. How much gold did you get?"

"Never you mind! It's all mine since you won't stay with me! An old lady like me needs a bit for a rainy day." Paul barely suppressed a snort as he looked at her. Old lady indeed! He suddenly realised how much she had changed from the time he first saw her, back in the Dark. Then, she looked - and sounded - like an old hag. Now, she was not old, nor ugly, now. She was quite the opposite. He had no idea what might have brought about such a transformation. Only her voice remained unchanged. Harsh and whining it was, and not much better now. A great pity, he thought, for although he was determined to find Moira, and, particularly, go to where she was, he was not averse to a little bit on the side.

Her sharp voice broke the train of thought. "Where you goin' then, if you're not staying here?" Paul had to tell her what he had seen in just a few brief moments. He told her of the beauty, the peace, the friends, and a hundred other things that seemed to pop up from nowhere.

"You're pulling my leg!" Jane scoffed, "Ain't nothin' like that! Not anywhere!"

"I didn't know myself," Paul insisted, "But while we were there together, all sorts of pictures showed her in gardens, marvellous buildings, different somehow. All just in a flash. I saw it, and I know it's true!"

Jane looked doubtfully at him. "I ain't never heard of any place like that, unless it's the real Heaven." She pondered a moment; then her eyes lit up. "Maybe...maybe it is! You think it could be?"

"I haven't the faintest idea," Paul grimaced, "I've never believed in Heaven. That's supposed to be the place you go when you die. Well, we're dead, aren't we?" Jane nodded, "I s'pose so." He went on, "Well, this is definitely not Heaven. It's not too bad here, and that's a hell of a lot better than where we were with that bully Billy. And that wasn't Heaven. That would be more like Hell, I suppose, but I don't know. But Moira told me I wasn't ready to go where she is, and I want to know why. Who makes the rules? Who tells me I can't go there?" He strode up and down, trying to understand what it was all about.

There was a gap between what must be fiction, as the popular picture of the Hereafter taught and promulgated on Earth, and the actuality as they were experiencing here and now, in this realm of perpetual day, neither hot nor cold, no hunger, no thirst, and clothing that came from nowhere, and then, somewhere over the rainbow, was this other, beautiful place.

He had to find it. At least, he had to try.

"Take me with you!" Jane rose as she spoke and stood beside him, enticing him with an unconscious wriggle of her hips. "Two's better than one, and who knows, we might find this place. Wot you say?"

Paul found her proximity unexpectedly inviting. "Yes," he thought, "She IS very attractive. And suppose I can't find Moira, or ever get to that Emerald City place…" Jane held out her hand. "You can have half of this, if you take me with you!" He looked at her open hand. There were six sovereigns gleaming at him. That, and her thigh pressing against him, was enough.

"Alright! We'll go together. But I'm the boss! You'll have to do what I say!" She nodded, "You're the boss, as long as you keep me safe and sound. Shake!" and she extended her free hand. They shook hands, but Paul had a sudden desire for more. He pulled her to him and embraced her passionately. Jane managed to free herself and gave a little laugh.

"OO! Who's the randy one then? You don't have to rape me to get it, like, no need to get rough!"

They dallied a little while which somehow, without any real planning, stretched out for some time. It did not matter; they had all eternity before them. When they emerged, Paul was more relaxed than he had been.

He looked up and down, pondering on which might be the best way to go. There was no way, whatever, of guessing how far they might have to go, let alone the direction. One way Paul was determined they would not be going! The direction which landed him in trouble after he left the tavern the first time. No, most certainly not that way!

"Do you think," he looked at Jane, "it's brighter over there" He pointed. Jane gave a little grimace, "I dunno, ducky. Maybe it is. You want to go that way?"

"Anyway, so long as it's the right way! So, what say we try that way?" She nodded. "You're the boss, ducky!" He took her arm, "To Oz?" She looked blankly at him. "Oz? What's Oz? I ain't never heard of that. Where's that?" Jane was puzzled.

"You know, follow the yellow brick road, and all that stuff! Emerald City?" Jane still looked blank. "I dunno wot you're on about! Oz! Emerald City!? Then Paul woke up. He realised the story of OZ was probably not known in Edwardian England. He gave her a quick outline, and while it was quite inane, they found a common ground in the fable and even enjoyed keeping it before them. So off they went, looking for the Emerald City in the Land of Oz

"Is this the right way?" Jane asked after a little while, "Ain't nothin' happenin' at all. But at least it's not raining. Least, I ain't seen any here yet."

"That's right," Paul replied thoughtfully, "No rain, no cold - no heat either - no night! It makes me wonder who dreamed all this up!" Jane had no answer. The urgency of living was much more important to her than the trivia of death or what comes after. Food, a decent place to sleep, and a full bottle of gin were much more useful than airy-fairy twaddle. None of that stuff filled a belly or cuddled you nice and cosy. True, she had a very hazy knowledge of religion, which to her meant Christianity, but that buttered no buns. If you went along and sang Jesus loves me or something, a very thin scrape of butter might appear on a miserable scrap of bread, but they made you stay off the gin.

How to survive and stay one jump ahead of the Law was enough for her. She had been a cut above the average street girl, and many of her clients were well-to-do gentlemen about town, so she was well accustomed to a lot of blather way over her head. She didn't care; it was not her mind they were interested in, and they paid well.

As they walked along, Paul was keeping a good lookout. He wanted no surprises. Jane, busy thinking about old times, left it all to him. The way was quite smooth, with trees, shrubs, a house or two, and plenty of people, going about whatever, they were doing, paying scant attention to anyone near them. They passed seemingly unnoticed, mainly because they did nothing other than go peacefully, even casually, by. Paul could not help wondering if the cudgel he carried was enough to pay their way, although it was not carried so as to be a threat; it was loosely slung over his shoulder.

This was going on for such a time that he wondered if anyone was seeing them at all. Determined to test it, he went up to a man and tapped him on the shoulder. The man spun around, and before he knew what hit him, Paul was on his back in the dust, with the man standing over him with a raised fist. It took a few moments to realise what had happened and why he had been floored. He carefully – and slowly - sat up and extended both hands in what he hoped was a peace gesture.

"I didn't mean to surprise you! I come in peace…" "Yeah? Looks like it, with that bloody great club!" Paul shook his head. "No, no! You've got it wrong! I carry that only in case I need it! And that is often, by the look of it!"

"What do you want, anyway, sneaking up on people like that? You don't do that around these parts!" "I meant no harm! We're strangers here! All I wanted, was to ask you where this road goes." The man slowly lowered his fist, "Alright! You can get up. But watch it! There's plenty of us here to wipe you out!" Only slightly less belligerent, he scratched his head. "I dunno where it goes. You'll have to ask someone else." As he spoke, he was leering at Jane, "A nice bit of stuff you got yourself! Care to trade? You can have my old woman...."; A scream from inside the nearby hut, a flash of a streaking figure descended on the man and turned on him with a barrage of blows from a broom wielded by a furious woman. "Swap me, would you? For that tart? I'll give you what for. You...You..." She ran out of tirade as she turned to the pair, "Go on! Get! Get out of here" "Go on! Get!"

They took her advice. They got. For some little time, they could hear the woman screaming, with the man trying to calm her, saying he was only kidding, they looked at each other, and then both collapsed in helpless laughter. Eventually, Paul wondered why a man tied himself to a woman spanning not one lifetime, but this one as well! Also, why were these people so ignorant? The man showed no curiosity as to where the road led. Was his life so full and complete as to want for nothing? Paul knew there were better things. Somewhere. HE WAS certain all he had to do was to keep looking. There had to be a way to get to this place somewhere, somehow.

Jane went along willingly enough for a start but soon became bored with just trailing along. There was little of interest anywhere, other than the man and his wife. "How much further do we have to go?" She felt like she had been walking forever. "When are we going to find this place? I'm tired of this!" She sat down on a rock, stretched, yawned, and looked glum. Paul stood, looking up and down, trying to gauge their progress, if any. The path was quite clearly defined but didn't seem to be used much. For all that, he was sure the light was brighter, and the greenery was more active, more alive than before.

While he was looking about, Jane fell to pondering a few things on her own. Why, for example, had she not been upset over Eve going off with someone? They were friends or had been up till then. Perhaps they were meant to part. And for all her feeling bored and tired, she felt that somehow, she would benefit from this search; how, that was unclear. There was something in what Paul had said before they had started out; she couldn't remember. But there was that deep feeling, that twinge, that 'something'.

Once, not long after she and Eve had arrived here -so long ago it seemed - they had been met by a nice person who asked them if they knew what had happened to them. Of course, at that time, they did not. This lady explained that they were now in the realm of spiritual life and that their bodies had died, but they, being spiritual entities- she didn't know what that meant - could not die. Eve had immediately laughed in derision, saying she couldn't be dead, but that any talk of spirits was flirting with the Devil. She told her to shove off and not come bothering decent folk.

Jane had listened to what the lady said, and somehow, she knew she was right. But Eve pulled her away, and there was no further chance to ask her anything. She must ask Paul about it. "Spirit being?" he frowned, "What made you ask that?" "Oh, it's just something a lady once said, just after me and Eve got here, in this place. She said we was spirit...something because we was dead. Is that right?"

"Funny!" Paul sat beside her, "When we arrived – Moira and I, a man called Thomas said the same thing. I've been trying to work it out ever since. He said that when someone dies, all that happens is that their body stops working, but the person, like you and me, keeps going. I don't understand it because we have bodies. He said something else, but I wasn't listening very hard, and I don't know now what it was."

"Anyhow, I'm sure we're making some progress because the trees are bigger and better, somehow, and there's a bird or two. So, we carry on. Only," He stretched, "I'm feeling a bit tired too, so let's take a rest. There's a little shelter over there, under that tree."

They were in the realm of Spirit alright, as spiritual beings, but Paul was a recent enough arrival that he had not outgrown his old circadian rhythm. So, they enjoyed a rest. When they awoke, it took a little while to recognise where they were. There was not a soul in sight, and this was unusual. He stretched and wondered why he wasn't hungry. However, a little tinkle nearby invited him to drink. The water was wonderful. Clean, clear, deliciously cool, and something else. As he drank, a feeling of well-being, of life, of energy flowed throughout his body. Although it had no discernible taste or flavour, he felt as if it were an elixir, a magic potion.

He discovered later that the air had the same magical properties, though not so pronounced. Jane came over and crouched beside him. "What are you doing?" Paul grinned at her. "Here! Drink some of this!" He pointed to the stream. She scooped up a little, drank it, and gave a little shiver. "Oooo!" Her eyes sparkled, "Oh, It's just like gin. No! Better!" She took another handful and swallowed it.

"Oh, I like this place! Free booze!"

"Good, isn't it!" Paul agreed, "It's very nice, but you find you won't want too much. Just enough to feel good and fresh. Better than gin, as you said, and it makes you feel fit and brighter, somehow" He stood up and grabbed her hand. "Come on! I get the feeling we don't have far to go now. This stream is so good I can't help wondering if it comes from - from where we're going. So come on." He pulled her along as he walked eagerly towards what he was sure was The Place. There was an urgency in his steps, for he was now certain the area ahead was brighter. He was right, for a few steps more brought a rapid change before them. Suddenly the light was almost blinding and extended across their full field of vision, with the place from where they had come dark, almost black by comparison.

Then Paul stopped suddenly, his mouth open with astonishment. As if a curtain had been pulled aside, there it was. They were looking at unimaginable beauty. It began right there, where they stood, and opened up before them, a vista of delight, of wondrous coloured flowers, lovely birds floating about, a path winding its way into the distance, all bathed in a serenity, a peace undreamt of.

They stood, completely entranced. At last, Jane whispered, afraid of breaking the spell, "Is it real? Is this the place you saw?"

"I suppose it must be," he whispered back, "but I can't see any city. Can you?" "No!" She answered, "Do you think we could…" "Go on?" "Yes, let's go on!" Although she said it, he knew from her trembling that she was really quite reluctant to do so. He tried to step forward, but a dream-like Deja vu caught him, just like the dream where you must move but cannot, as something turns your strength to nothing. He could not move.

"I...I can't!" he said in a hoarse whisper, a little panic creeping in.

"Neither can I!" She gripped his arm, "It's as if I shouldn't, like

I'm not good enough. I feel – I dunno – Like I done something wrong! But I been good! Well, mostly!"

"That's right! I feel the same, but also, I feel as if I'm exposed, and if I go, everyone will know all about me. I've done nothing really wrong - well, not much. I don't feel ready…"

The sudden realisation of what Moira had said brought an understanding of what she meant.

"Come on. We've got to go back!" He led the way back to the little glade where they had rested. Slumping down on the rock, he groaned. "What are we going to do now? We can't go on. I suppose we'll have to go back to the tavern." Jane sat beside him and threw her arms around him. "Don't be upset, ducky! We got each other, we got a bit o' brass, and it's not so bad here. Wot you say?"

Paul barely heard her. He was busy with his own thoughts. "Moira said I wasn't ready. That's right, damn it! I don't feel ready. Does that mean there's something I have to do, or learn, maybe?" A voice interrupted him. He looked up to see John, the one who had met them after the crash. He was saying,

"That's right, Paul. There is something you have to do. I cannot tell you what it is; it's part of your progress that you must discover that yourself." Paul shot to his feet angrily.

"Bloody Hell! Is that all you came to tell me? Is this a bloody great game, where I have three guesses, and I get the prize? What crap is this?" John smiled gently, "It looks like it, but no, Paul, it's simply a matter of your spiritual advancement. This goes for everyone on this plane..." Paul burst in. "So, there's a caste system here, is there? We're not good enough for the next realm, is that it? I'm as good as anyone else and a damn sight better than most!" John replied, his soft voice calm and sincere. "Your worth here is never a measure of your standing back on Earth. You have no doubt heard the old saying about the camel going through the eye of a needle before a rich man can enter the Kingdom of Heaven. Well, that is quite true, except that it is not quite Heaven. So, wealth and social position have nothing to do with it."

John continued, "The coin, you might say, is based simply on your attitude towards others and how far you will go on their behalf. So, if you feel you qualify, so to speak, you may try again to enter that realm. It's always up to the individual; nobody will test you, nobody will pass judgement. Only you can do that, and only you know when you are ready and able."

As he spoke in his quiet voice, with no trace of condescension or talking down, Paul slowly became calm again as his words sank in. He looked at John, slightly abashed. "What do I do now, then? I'm sorry I got mad just now; everybody keeps trying to tell me something I don't understand. All I seem to do is bash my head against a wall!"

"You have a good companion; go with her and see if you can work along the lines I was talking about - your attitude towards others and a desire to help them. I need tell you no more, but if you do get into serious trouble, I might be able to help. I'm not a fairy godfather, but I do have some tricks I can pull!"

The moment he finished speaking, he was gone. Paul could only stare at where he had been. He turned to Jane, "Did you get any of that? What the Hell is it all about? He sounded like a Bible-Basher with his camels and needles. All these guys do is preach!"

Jane surprised him with her reply. "Yes, ducks, it did alright! But that man sounded just like a feller who used to preach to us, oh, way back when I was a snotty kid. He spoke like that, but it wasn't the same as the others. They raved about hellfire and purgatory, but he never. He talked about, you know, kindness, helping others even if it costs something."

"It made you feel good when he talked, and I always tried to go when he was on. The others tried to scare us, but this one, he was one of the Sallys; he made you want to go and hug someone. I think I loved him, and I was only ten. He never talked about Jesus, or sins, or Hell, only about being kind and gentle. This fella, here just now, he was like him!"

Paul sat and stared at her. What could he say to that? There was an old lady, now looking more in her late twenties, a confessed prostitute, telling him stuff he had scorned as a boy. He had always said that you never get anywhere by being nice. Kindness was for idiots - soft in the head, or wimps. And she was backing up what John had said. Then another thought made him stop. John may be kind and helpful, but he is most certainly not a wimp.

Just for a brief glimpse, Paul was able to see something of what this was all about. He almost had it, but his old views intruded, and he lost the one train of thought that might lead him to the Emerald City. All he could say was, "I don't understand. This is all beyond me. So, what do we do now?'

"Don't be sad, ducky" Jane sat down beside him and tried to cheer him up. "Maybe we can find a town somewhere. Eve always said there was a village near us, but we never found it."

"I don't want any bloody village!" He shouted angrily, 'We've just seen this place, just as I saw with Moira, and I'm going there, come hell or high water, I'm going!"

Jane looked at him thoughtfully. She could see a helpless, spoiled child who was always given what he wanted, or a fierce tantrum resulted. She also saw a sensitive, considerate, loving young man lying dormant, awaiting the right situation to trigger it, to bring it forth. Gently she kissed him.

"We'll find a way; you see if we don't! You got brains and education - you see if we don't!" Paul looked at her, still angry but softened by her encouragement.

He stood up and paced to and fro, pounding a fist into a palm. Then in a sudden decision, he pulled Jane to her feet.

"Come on! Let's give it another try! I can't just sit here after only one attempt. Let's see if we can find out just what stopped us." Jane already knew, and he had been told by John, but it had not sunk in. However, she went along with him, not wanting to aggravate his mood.

Further, she increasingly saw in him someone who needed helping. She had listened carefully to what John had said, and that, along with the long-forgotten lesson of her childhood, had brought about the spiritual awakening long delayed by her previous associations.

She knew what had stopped them. John had given her the clue, so long buried under all the myths and legends taught by the different Christian churches. Later she was to learn why the real truth was buried. Just now, it was enough to fully realise what had happened after that fire so long ago.

She and Eve arrived together and, of course, could not accept their state of being. They were spiritually dead as well as physically so. And they were not in a very pleasant area, which was, of course, in keeping with their attitude to others. There were cheats, rogues, and many other unsavoury people. They were in good company. The lady who visited them would have helped, but Eve knew best. Jane was now certain that Eve's closed mind - in common with the others there – had kept them in that horrible place. At that time, she accepted it, knowing no better. Now, she wondered at her stupidity. John had opened her eyes.

She was a spirit being and always had been. Her advancement was in her own hands. She could make or mar her future by her own actions. She knew that she - anyone - had to feel at home in the higher realms; it had to feel right. By service and thoughtfulness to others, this could be brought about. Only one small factor remained hidden; there was help available, every moment, everywhere - all one had to do was ask. As yet, no-one had told her that.

This time, they had barely gone fifty metres when they reached the point dividing the two realms. There, through a haze of brilliance, they could see the spires, towers, and domes of a cluster of buildings, iridescent and glowing, breathtaking in their beauty. Paul could not restrain a gasp of wonder.

"Will you look at that! I've never imagined anything like it! Look at the path!!" Indeed, the dim trail they had been following was now a handsome paved pathway, winding its way to the city.

Jane gripped his arm as she exhaled a long-drawn-out sigh, "Ooooh! I've never seen anything so lovely! It's more beautiful than I thought!" "Yes, and I'm going! Are you coming?" Jane had little choice as he dragged her with him. He strode forward grimly determined.

But he could go no further. Held by that ghastly dream-like scene of one in dire trouble but unable to move. He could not make his leaden feet obey. He clutched at Jane in his effort to take that step forward. Oddly enough, he was not afraid, for there was nothing to fear, just that horrible paralysis of his legs. He knew this would defeat him – it always did in a dream. In the dream, it would not matter; he was bound to wake up shortly in his room back in Wellington. Then he could shrug off the whole episode, Billy the bully and all.

At this point, his strength deserted him, and he sank to the ground, praying that he would indeed wake up. Some little time later, he became aware of Jane bending over him, pleading for him to come back to her, to answer her. His legs felt normal, the discomfort gone.

"What the hell happened" He groaned as he sat up. "Did I pass out? I just had a horrible dream…"

"Oh, you're alright!" She clutched him. "Oh, I thought I had lost you! Can you die if you're already dead?"

"I dunno" Paul shook his head, trying to understand what had just happened. "How did I get back here? I was over there, and couldn't move a muscle…"

"You just fell down, like you dropped dead! But I knew, somehow – I dunno, that you weren't. I could move. I don't know why you couldn't, but I was able to drag you back here. But… Jane forestalled him, "I know you're too heavy for me to …" She grabbed him around his waist and lifted. "See, you're light!" She hugged him close to her. "I've still got you. That's all that counts," she cried. "I couldn't bear to lose you!"

They stood in each other's arms, enjoying the comfort shared as they both regained their composure. Paul looked in the direction now closed to them and groaned through clenched teeth.

"Why? Why can't we go there? Why? Why?" "Paul!" She stroked his face, "It's because there is a lot to learn, to well, to grow somehow. But it's us, just us! Like the man who came to us a little while ago said, we've got a lot to learn…"

But he was still too upset by what he construed as a rebuff from some unknown force, as if scorning his puny efforts to better himself. He smarted under the imagined insult.

"I feel so inadequate!" He glared at the brightness ahead, and the invisible block. "If that's the way it is, they can keep it! We'll just go our own way!"

Don't be upset; she coaxed him. "Who knows what might be just around the corner!"

He gripped her hand, still upset, but never-the-less accepting her comfort. Her touch was soothing enough that in a little while, he kissed her, stood up, pointed, and said,

"Come on! If we must learn, let's go and learn! But where the Hell we'll go? I haven't the slightest idea. So, let's try this way." Taking her firmly by the hand, he led off across the little glade to where a faintly outlined path led off, in the general direction of the little stream.

It was easy travelling, with pleasant vistas opening up here and there. All was quiet and tranquil. This was because They were unaware that they were skirting along the boundary between the two realms. And, of course, this was why they met no one. They were in an area shunned by the lower regions, as they felt too exposed. And the higher-level dwellers had little cause to come here, so they travelled alone.

"They found it easy to keep going; they were not tiring. Hopefully, they would find a place of interest before long. Then they noticed a sudden increase in the width of the stream; it was now several metres wide, caused, Paul, surmised, by their little rill joining a larger one.

Jane stopped walking, "I hear singing! Over there! She pointed. Paul agreed, "Yes, over there, to our left!"

He approached the stream, "It's quite shallow; we'll have to wade across. Can you swim?" "No, I can't! I'll get all wet! You'll have to carry me? She had the Cockney fear of water. Paul looked into the clear water, perhaps half a metre deep.

"Ok, then, come on! And don't jiggle, or I'll drop you!"

First, she tried to mount piggyback, but her skirt got in the way. Then he picked her up in his arms, found she was a lightweight, and stepped into the water. The first few paces were fine, but he couldn't see where he was putting his feet. And it happened. He slipped, tried to regain his balance, failed, and the pair finished up sitting midstream in waist-deep water.

"Look what you've done!" Jane wailed, "Look! I'm soaked!" But it was not so. On Earth, when you fall into water, you get wet. Here, you don't. In amazement, she stood up, and the water ran off her clothes, and they were quite dry. "Hey! Will you look at that! Dry! The water just runs off!" She giggled in surprise and splashed the water about, watching it sparkle.

"Come on, let's see if we're dry when we get out" This time, she did the leading, and the remainder of the crossing was quickly made. As they thought, they were completely dry. Paul slowly shook his head in disbelief. Just another unexpected side of this place.

Jane noticed it first. She was looking around, trying to locate where the singing, now stopped, had come from. "Oh, look!" She pointed. There was a bridge, hidden by the curve in the river. She laughed. "If we had found the bridge, we wouldn't have found out about the water!"

A subtle change had taken place in Jane. He tried to spot it; he thought she was much softer, more feminine, more perceptive, and a much more desirable companion. She seemed to have shed her background; she was no longer a whore. He shook his head wryly. More questions that needed answers. Maybe someone over where the singing had come from could help, after all his tantrums.

"Come on," he took her hand, "Let's see if we can find this place." Jane acknowledged with a little squeeze.

From the belatedly discovered bridge, a path led off, meandering through the trees. They had not far to go. Around the bend was a high wall with houses visible behind it. Paul correctly guessed the wall surrounded the houses, with a gate – open - in the wall in front of them. They could see down into the village, and by what they saw, it seemed clean and tidy, with a few well-dressed people visible. They looked at each other, trying to decide whether to enter, when a voice called out.

"Hullo, strangers! Welcome to Salem!" The voice belonged to a thick-set man with a cheerful face. He was dressed in eighteenth-century garb, pantaloons, a frock coat, tricorn hat, complete with a wig. "Come in and rest! We offer you our humble hospitality," He beckoned them.

"Come on, don't be afraid. We are all good folk here." The man looked friendly enough, and with no valid reason for refusing, they walked forward. The man came up as they entered.

My name is Jacob, and I am the town elder. We are a happy little parish here. You are most welcome to stay with us. I must ask," He paused, doubt on his face, "Your clothes are unusual. Are you from these parts?"

Paul had no reason to say other than no, and added, "We are seeking knowledge. We hoped there would be someone here who could help us."

"That depends," The man called Jacob frowned, "That depends on what you seek. Your companion, does she seek as well? Methinks her dress is as strange as yours. He turned to Jane, "Where did you say you hail from? Jane looked startled at being spoken to but managed to splutter...

"I lived in London. Is that a crime? She clutched Paul's arm for protection, although the man seemed pleasant enough. But there was something about him that was vaguely disquieting. He looked friendly enough, like a good, solid citizen, but he seemed a little false, a shade too affable.

A small crowd had gathered around them, and Jacob turned to them and asked, "Shall we welcome these two strangers, who come in search of knowledge?" and murmurs of agreement answered him.

They were uniformly dressed in black, with no colour, no adornments, and Paul thought, no spirit. They were drab and lifeless.

He had to wonder how spirit beings could appear so dead. These did. Were they prisoners? Or were they in the grip of somebody? Jacob? He didn't think so; he felt it would be someone else, because, if this was any reflection of the Earth-plane, the big cheese would appear only to impress and perhaps intimidate and command. To be too readily available, too convivial, would lower his standing.

Therefore, he would hold himself aloof. And these people looked subdued. He was right, but when he realised it, he was far too late. Inconspicuous and smooth, several heavies had slowly worked their way through the small throng and now stood behind them. Paul could not suppress a small shudder of apprehension. As casually as he could, he said, "We thank you for your offer, but we have some urgent business to attend to." He knew it was hopeless, but he had to try.

The gate clanging shut behind them said it all. It was quite useless to attempt to cut and run; That would mean leaving Jane behind, for he had no idea of whether she could run, and those skirts were no help.

"We have closed the gates for safety," Paul was sure he was lying, "There are many evil men out there," Jacob said solemnly, "We must fight a long hard battle to bring them to the Lord, as we all belong to the Lord here. Are you God's children or the Devil's?"

Paul remembered what Thomas had said - how long ago? - that everyone was a child of God, although he didn't think that was what Jacob wanted. However, as far as he knew, he was not lying when he said they belonged to God, and he hoped fervently that he was not to be drawn into a theological discussion; he would lose hands down.

"I'm very glad that's your answer. We cannot allow any disciples of Satan in our midst!" Paul had been trying to place these people and their Earth-plane origin. Now, he thought he had it. While he was at university, he had been briefly interested in early North American history. He had studied the Pilgrim Fathers who had fled England to escape religious persecution, only to set up their own brand of religious tyranny on arriving in the New World.

He had to ask if this was so. Jacob took a noble stance and declaimed, "We are all Puritans here! We all came here to escape the evils of the Roman church pretending to be the Church of England! We have settled here to bring this Godless place into the fold! It is our duty to seek out and punish the Ungodly."

Paul had been right. These people had been completely subjugated in the Name of God. His heart sank as he looked about. How could he have been so stupid? A marvellous thing, hindsight, he thought bitterly. His heart sank still further as he realised the name of the village. It was Salem. And it would be, without any doubt, named after Salem, Massachusetts.

He bent over, pretending to straighten Jane's hat, and whispered, "We've got to get out of here! Fast!" She whispered back, 'But they're not bad people, are they?" "You don't understand! They burn witches at Salem, or did, back on Earth."

"What mischief are you plotting? What are you saying, talking secretly with your – your…" "My wife," Paul finished for him, "We were just wondering if we might rest a while, and then we'll continue with our quest." Jacob stepped closer and peered into their faces.

"There's something strange about you two," he peered again, "We will have to take you to Brother Elija. He will know about you, and he will decide if you are pure." He signalled to the heavies, who grabbed the pair and marched them down the path to a bigger, more impressive building than the others. They knocked, and the door opened, revealing a well-furnished room with a large desk under a window. "So," thought Paul, "This is where the big cheese is. He can't be as bad as Billy the Butcher. Or can he? Surely, he can't accuse us of being witches. Can he?" They were paraded before the desk and told to stand and wait. The two guards stood watchfully by as Paul, as casually as he could, looked about, trying to weigh up their chances. Once again, he thought he might make it; the guards were not very bright looking. But again, he immediately threw that idea away, for he was not about to abandon Jane.

Further, thought was cut off as a large, imposing, solemn man entered and sat at the desk. Paul knew the trick; his back was now to the window, and Paul could not see his face clearly - a well-known device to place visitors at a disadvantage. "So! What have we here?" It was a no-nonsense voice, totally in command. Paul immediately – and correctly dubbed him as a despot. He thought it might be prudent to butter him up a bit, that is, if it would work.

"We are wayfaring strangers, with malice towards none, and a deep abiding faith in Almighty God. We come in peace, and desire to depart, also in peace." The man sat, immobile, looking impassively at Paul. He appeared to be waiting for Paul to go on, but he had tossed the ball back, and it was his turn. And although the man made no threat, there was something dangerous about him.

At last, he looked at Jane. "Are you truly with this man? You seem very different from each other. Are you, his wife?" This was a man, who, by his questioning manner, was well accustomed to grilling his hapless victims, and Paul was sure they would pay a hefty price for any loose answers.

"Yes, of course, she is!" Paul had to interject; he had to speak up to give Jane a lead. "Silence," the man thundered, "I was asking her! Have the goodness to remain silent unless spoken to! Now!" He turned back to Jane, "Are you, his wife? And don't lie!" but Paul's intervention had been timely; she had got the message, "Of course, we're married! You don't think I would travel about with a man who was not my husband!" "I don't believe you!" the man said with great authority, "First, where is your ring? Second, your manner of dress is more like a Jezebel, and certain to be inspired by Satan!"

"But Sir," Paul was seething, but was determined not to allow this man the upper hand, "Sir, may I speak?" The man slowly turned to Paul and glared intimidatingly. Paul stood his ground.

'Very well. You may speak, for all the good that will do!" Elija replied.

"Sir, you lived in the eighteenth century, did you not?" The man looked puzzled. "What's that got to do with it? I'm still alive, and it's still seventeen hundred and fifty something; I'm not sure. So, what are you talking about?"

"Sir, we were born in the Twentieth century, two hundred years later than you. So, our clothes are different; our speech is different..." Elija slammed his fist down on the desk.

"I've never heard such lies! I shall have to investigate in case you are indeed talking heresy! How can you stand there and say you are two hundred years younger than me? Or is it older? I don't know; you're talking about impossibilities!" He sat a moment glaring at them. Finally, he roused and waved his hand. "Take them away while I ponder what to do with these - these liars who come here upsetting our simple life!"

Paul managed to get in a parting shot. He murmured, "God moves in mysterious ways His wonders to perf...."

Elija pricked up his ears, "What's that? What did you say?" Paul repeated it, louder this time. Elija slumped back in surprise. Seeing the effect, he had made, he tried another. "Do you know any Shakespeare, Sir? He said, there are more things 'twixt Heaven and Earth than are dreamed of in your philosophy!"

But that was the wrong quotation. Elija reared up and growled, "He was an ungodly man and should be punished! Even if what he said is true, he deserves the Wrath of God!" He turned and walked out, saying as he went, "Take them away! I will ask divine guidance and will then decide what to do."

Outside, Paul was jerked in one direction and Jane in the other. Speechless for a moment, he stared. Jane was being hustled out of sight around the corner of a building. All he could do was call after her, "I'll get us out, somehow!" He struggled to follow her, but it was no use. They dragged him towards another building further away.

"Why are we being held prisoner? We've done you no harm." Jacob signalled his men to stop, "We told you that it's dangerous out there!" He waved towards the fence, "We must in Christian charity protect you, and to do that, we must be sure you are true believers."

But Paul had more questions. "So you say. We've come a long way out there, and we came to no harm whatever! But why have you taken my wife away? We belong together!" Jacob intoned pompously, "Men must not live with women! If they are together, they will sin, and sinning is not permitted."

Paul stared at him. He was on the verge of howling with laughter, but he realised Jacob was not joking. He had to wonder if Jacob had been born of an immaculate conception. He asked, "Did your parents commit a sin to beget you?"

Jacob stepped back in confusion. This was something he had never considered. These people had minds completely shut off from the normal run of things usually considered Reality. He had met bigots before this but never of this incredible depth. Also, he was sure this would have come from Brother Elija, irrational but strong.

"It will pay you, brother, to keep such dreadful thoughts to yourself," Jacob attempted to regain his composure, "There is a sore trial ahead of you. If you are indeed devout, you will spend time in prayer. Now, in you go!"

He was pushed firmly into a cubicle, the door slammed shut and locked before he could even turn around. In the dim light, he saw what looked like a figure sitting on a bench along one wall. He asked a trifle anxiously, "Hullo! Is there anyone there?"

"Hullo, Paul!" A pleasantly deep voice answered. "Welcome to our little gaol!" The figure stood up and approached him. "You don't know me, but I hope you soon will. I've been sent to keep an eye on you; we don't want you to come to any harm. My name is Sean, and I can help in many ways you probably have never heard of." The voice was soft, assured, with a little chuckle barely concealed below it.

He extended his hand to Paul, who took it numbly. So much had happened, so quickly, that from the time he had crossed that stream with Jane, until now, it all seemed a blur. The man called Sean led him to the bench and sat down.

"Now, I think you are in a frame of mind to understand a little about life here in the spirit realms. As I said, we've been watching you, and we have no intention of allowing any harm to come to you. That's why I'm here, as well as to fill in all these gaps you have. Now, we'll have plenty of time to talk!" He spread his hands in invitation, "So! Fire away with all the questions I know you have!"

Moira at School

Moira emerged from her first session in the projection room, dazed, elated, and tired but happy. She was not quite sure which of those was uppermost. She had just enjoyed a long history lesson. This had taken place in a room, completely featureless, with nothing but several chairs in the centre. The floor, wall, and ceiling were all white, and it was impossible to tell where the walls and floor met.

She had been introduced to the room by her tutor, a pleasant young man who said his name was Arthur. He had brought her in, sat her down, and, sitting next to her, made a signal to someone to begin. They had decided to see something not too disturbing for a start. She had thought that perhaps she could see something like the Battle of Hastings, but Arthur had wisely talked her out of that; she would have been overwhelmed and shocked. Those battles were not nice.

She settled for Armstrong and Aldrin, whose names are always remembered by space buffs. Arthur gave a little chuckle as an expression of anticipation flashed across his face. Moira should have been warned by this, but there was no time. In a heartbeat, the chamber disappeared. She was out in space, a soft velvety space. Over on her right was the breathtakingly beautiful sight of Mother Earth, looking like a Goddess. Before her, and below, was the Moon. The view swept forwards and down until she was skimming along over craters, mountain peaks, ravines, and finally stopped beside a small crater.

Above, she saw the flame of a rocket slowing the space capsule as it dropped, alarmingly at first and then gently wafting down, barely dodging the crater as it came. Enthralled, she watched as a clumsy figure emerged and climbed slowly down to take that "Giant Leap for Mankind."

Entranced, she watched as Buzz Aldrin followed Neil Armstrong to the lunar surface and the antics performed for an audience of many millions back on Earth. She was THERE. She could feel the chair, its seat, and its arms, but she was there. Totally. She began to appreciate why Arthur had asked her to choose something a little less violent than the Battle of Hastings. Then, finally, she witnessed the departure of the little capsule leaving behind the various instruments and things of space research, allowing the peace of eternity to return.

As suddenly as she left, she was back in the chamber. The lunar scene was replaced by the white walls. She felt disorientated and not a little bewildered. It took a few moments to recover from the incredible experience of being on the surface of the Moon, totally and indelibly. She let out a long whoosh of breath.

"How do you do that? Did we actually go to the Moon? It was so real!" "As real as not to know the difference," Arthur smiled, "I told you what to expect, but the experience is something else!" She let out another long breath, "Is it Ever!" She sat for a few moments savouring the lingering remnants of what she had just seen.

"Is it all like that? That was real enough, I think; a battle would be a bit much!" "A bit much! Ha! A bit much, she says! And yes, it's all like that. This room is actually circular with a transparent floor. We cannot tell how big it is, but that doesn't matter. The scenes we see are taken from the complete records we have here. Everything that has happened, and I mean everything, is recorded in the warp and weft of the cosmos. That includes all the physical universe, as well as all the higher realms. We have some means I don't understand of bringing it up to be displayed here, just as though you are there. That's all I know."

"But the most important use of these rooms - yes, there are many, is to encourage you to scan back through your past lives on Earth, to refresh your memory of who you were, and more particularly, what you did, and what lessons you have learnt. This will be of great value to you as you will then be able to plan your future better."

"You mean," Moira asked in disbelief, "I have lived before this? Is it true, reincarnation and all that?"

"Yes, indeed, it is true, and regardless of what is taught in your previous halls of learning. Oh, I know many people feel they have lived before their current life, but there has been little support for it. Oh, yes, it's true, alright! Your immediate past life, in fact, all of them, have been for one or more reasons."

"One, is simply to learn something, some lesson. Another is for you to pay an old debt, or perhaps both reasons together. So, when you come back here after a lifetime, you need to know how you managed. That, you will find out, is one of the main uses of these rooms."

Moira looked at him. "I don't quite get what you mean. Is it like looking back through one's past?" "Precisely," Arthur nodded, "How do you feel if I ask you to scan back through your recent passing? Your death, as you might say?"

"Must I? That was horrible! Must I?

"No, you don't, but it would help you a great deal. You are never forced to do anything. What happens is always your own choice. So, what'll it be?"

After a moment, Moira nodded. "Good! We encourage everyone to do this; it helps you in ways I cannot tell you about in a few words. Remember, he added, "What you will see is only a memory. It is not occurring now; it's in your past."

Moira gave a little shudder. "Alright! I'll do it! If I think any more about it, I'll be too scared!"

As abruptly as before, the room vanished. Paul was driving the speeding car as it charged down the hill, shouting with glee as he believed they were catching the car in front. Then to her puzzlement, her viewpoint changed. Instead of looking from her body's eyes, she was behind Paul, pummelling his shoulder to no effect. Beside him was this other person screaming for him to slow down. It was some moments before she realised that it was her who was screaming. She was aware of the fuddled excitement of Paul as she desperately tried to reach his mind, aware of his frantic, insane attempts at being a racing driver, but she could not penetrate the alcoholic fog.

Then, at the moment of leaving the road, she was no longer in the car. Somehow, she saw it all happen from a point above them. She saw the car crash through the roadside fence and hurtle out and down, to land on its nose in the little gully. There was no pain, no body sensations - nothing. But here she was, still poised above the car, now a pile of junk. She could see it quite clearly and was also aware of a car that stopped on the roadway above and heard the voices raised in alarm.

Then she saw Paul emerge from the wreck, dazed but seemingly unhurt. She went down to him and started to berate him for his folly when Thomas and John arrived to take them to their cottage.

The entire episode was there, clear, sharp, all actions, all impressions. But nowhere was there pain or fear of impending death. She knew that her foremost thought was danger, apprehension, but it seemed someone else was experiencing this, not her. It was not until Thomas told her that she had died that she started to panic.

At that moment, the scene dissolved, and she was once again in the room with Arthur. "Now," she said, after a pause long enough for her to recover from the scene. She could not restrain her tears in the shock of recall. And she knew that her transition into this realm had been really very easy. So why do common mortals dread it so? She knew people were terrified of dying, but there was literally nothing in it! She dried her eyes with a wry thought, 'How does a spiritual being have tears?' Arthur smiled. He was understanding enough to know exactly how she felt. She caught the easy, relaxed support he was giving and squeezed his arm gratefully.

"Now," he said quietly, "If you feel recovered enough, let's go through that until we reach anything you didn't understand." "That's easy!" Moira laughed, easing the strain a little, "It was when I first found myself behind Paul. I could see myself sitting beside him, and now, seeing it again, I wonder how that could be possible. I mean, I was in two places at once. That's not possible, is it?"

"No. It isn't! You can't be in two places at once. What happens is that you, a being senior and able to be separated from your body, did just that. In an incident of real peril, inescapable danger, as you were, you may hop out of your body in alarm. In your case, of course, it was real. If you survive the threat to you, you will usually take up your body again. But all dying is the same, in that the 'being', such as you and I, always leaves the body, in this case, permanently. Your body is no longer of any use; it's been damaged beyond recovery."

"It just stops working, for reason of accident, sickness, or simple old age." He gave a little chuckle, "Of course, it's not unknown for someone to merely think the end is here and abandon a perfectly good body needlessly! You could say they've been frightened to death! The pity of all this is that so very few living on Earth know anything about this. They don't know they are spirit beings operating bodies; they are all told that they ARE the body! Only those curious enough really find out about it and understand what happens. When they do and try to tell others, they often meet guffaws, derision, and general abuse!"

"So, this is my soul, then? Is that right?" "Yes, in a way, that is right, but there's a great deal more to it than that. Just let's say, provisionally, yes, for the moment. There is much to learn yet. All your questions will be answered in time, first, about your transition. We don't call it death because you cannot die. Only the body you had can die. As it is made of earth minerals and compounds, and as you are not, you are senior to it."

He continued, "Without you, it is nothing but chemicals and water. You, the God-force, animates it." There is no life without Spirit. None. Nowhere. There are millions of spirit beings walking around the Planet Earth, unaware that they are anything but just bodies."

"Spirit is Life. Life is Spirit. They are inseparable. Perhaps you can now begin to understand something about yourself. Since all things come from the Infinite Creator, the one usually called God, but has other names; then all things are interconnected; the vastness of the Cosmos contains all the realms of Spirit along with the entire universe of matter, the only one recognised by humanity."

"Everywhere you look, from the heights of Heaven to the depths of Hell, you will find the hand of God. As I look at you, I can say, 'Thou art God!"

"I'm beginning to understand," Moira said slowly, "But can you tell me why I live again and again? I can't remember doing that. Surely once is enough. Have I got to go through all the agony of childhood again and again?"

"Questions! Questions! I know you must ask, and we must answer, but take it slower!"

This began many more sessions in the white chamber. She was to learn many things about Planet Earth, with surprises coming thick and fast. This made her more and more thirsty for more, and for reasons she could not explain, she was drawn more and more to humanity's religious history.

It was no surprise to learn that all such beliefs sprang from the ideas of primitive man in his efforts to relate to his environment. It was also no surprise to see how priesthood cults arose, where the people accepted their pretence at knowing it all, and how this was not long in burgeoning into the priests themselves becoming Holy men that common men must turn to as they had 'the' hotline to God.

A jealous leadership developed in which they only could talk to their God, and no-one else dared do so. And, of course, they demanded their tithes and more, in some cases, to support their privileged lifestyle. But underlying it all, she learnt how Man had a deep abiding yearning for real communication between himself and the one he regarded as the Almighty One, the Creator, the Comforter.

All too rarely in the upward struggle of Man, she leant of the few whose lives shone as beacons down through the ages and who invariably met fierce opposition from the priesthood of the day. Heretics, they were called. This was the practice down through the ages, and it is still going on. And in every case she could find, these heretics had something of immense value to say.

Some of these were from before any reliable records were kept. And while very interesting, Moira was drawn to names known more to her period, such as the Egyptian Osiris, Enoch, and Melchizedek, even the other Egyptian Akhnamon, who changed his name to Akhenaton, who tried to set up a monotheistic faith. Unfortunately, the movement died with him.

Then there were the Greeks, Socrates and Aristotle. They postulated the existence of a soul. Socrates was forced to take poison for his pains because he challenged the hierarchy. But around the same time, there was another who discovered that if he meditated deeply enough, he could actually separate himself from his body. He was Gautama Siddhartha, the Enlightened One, later known as the Buddha. And not surprisingly, she further learnt that once the priests became involved, they preached their own version, and it was little more than a vestige of the original.

Over many sessions, the historical pattern became established, and she was soon able to understand why Christianity had lost its following. In total absorption, she sat through the unfolding story. There were the Magi, the Zoroastrians, who were truly wise men! They knew of the coming of the child, who would bring Humanity into the light of understanding. She saw these wise men come and pay homage to the infant Jesus.

She watched - no became completely involved in – the journeyings of the young Jesus as he went to India and Tibet, where he studied with their wise men, and how he corrected an important error in their teaching. The myth that they believed about progressing through different life-forms, reincarnating as a beetle, a bird, or a pig, and so up to being a man. Jesus asked them if any could remember being an ant or a pig. None of them could. They insisted it was true because their priests told them. Then Moira was treated to a masterly lecture on Man's origin.

Firstly, she heard something she was often told - to take nothing she was told as knowledge. Knowledge, the master said, comes from one source, and one only, Experience. As you of all existence, Jesus went on, from when you first walked with Our Father God in the plane of soul, it is simply a matter of you casting your minds back to the land of Spirit when you will remember, for you never really forget.

"You will learn," he went on, that there never was a time when Man was not. If that were so, there will come a time when Man will be no more.

"We know, by reaching back, and searching The Book of God's Remembrance, that He, the All-Powerful, the All-Wise, the All-Loving God, breathed a mighty breath and brought forth seven spirits, who now stood before him."

"These seven, with the blessings of God, created all there is. Everything. They created the realms of Spirit wherein all beings were placed, in their different planes, and clothed them in the substance fitting to their creation."

"These planes are never seen by the eyes of matter or flesh because they are a much finer texture than our plane of matter, and all nourishment is drawn from the ethers of those planes."

"Then all the thoughts of God, and of the seven, as appearing on the planes of spirit, began to vibrate slower and slower, and all became denser, descending downward, becoming more gross, affecting all things, animal, vegetable and of course man."

"Thus, this plane, the Plane of Matter where we now find Man, along with all the other creations, now also of matter. Then, all the creations now on the Plane of Matter, could draw sustenance from the atmosphere, but the strongest turned on the weaker for nourishment, for food. From this arose the belief in the survival of the fittest and the concept of the food chain."

"So, shameless Man now kills for food any animal, the animal eats plants, and the plants feed on the Earth. This was not so, on the Plane of the Seven Spirits, as they were so shall they ever be."

"So, you see, a plant can never be a bird, a bird can never be a man, nor an ant, nor a spider. Likewise, Man is Man and can never be anything else but Man."

Moira went about in a daze for some time after that. While being only vaguely religious, she had been actually listening to a man many believed to be only a myth. She asked her tutor.

"Yes indeed, you have! But let me put you right on one small point. He is not Jesus Christ, but Jesus 'the' Christ. There is a difference, as you will learn. As for your other question about hearing him talk about things which are not in the Bible, that's something else to uncover."

They told her about how the Bible was compiled from many different writings, mostly chosen on the whims and fancies of those present. Further, they said, the parts you have just seen come straight from the record he mentioned - the Book of God's Remembrance, or as we often call it, the Akashic Record. This is the source of all she saw in the viewing chamber.

Moira was puzzled by another thing; what would have caused the ether in the Plane of Soul to vibrate slower and slower? If everything was perfect, with the creations of the Seven living in harmony and peace together, what really caused this thing which must be the fall of man?

"No, child, God made no mistake. As we see it from here, it went something like this: Man, being created in the image of God, had all the divine attributes of God, and the last attribute bestowed upon the newly-created Man was the power of choice, of a free will, operating within the framework of the cosmos."

"It is best to regard it like this… If you liken all this to a game, with a field, a set of rules, and purposes in the game, goals to attain. There are rules and regulations within the game, but there are many freedoms within the scope of the game. Freedoms within the laws. But Man had to learn about these things. In creating Man, God did not say why; He did not say until; He did not give any direction. He, being All-wise, knew that His creation had all the potential to discover, to grow. "Man had the power, but not the wisdom that must go together with the power."

As his knowledge of himself was almost nil, he misused his power, and by a law, he had yet to learn, the law of cause and effect, he lost some of that power."

"Yes," Moira objected, "But why? Why would that happen? I don't understand."

"First," the tutor replied, "You must realise that Man, for all the signs to the contrary, is basically good. This is because he has a conscience. At least, give him a chance, and he does! Probably his first discovery was that he could create things himself. He did this by thought power. Remember, he is made in the image of his Creator! With no inhibitions, no wisdom, but the power to create. And what he created would be visible to others. Then there would be a flurry of creating going on, all kinds of things, until the whole place became quite cluttered."

"Then, someone got the idea of breaking up his work by using some destructive thought at it, something like a beam of some kind. When he found this worked, others started as well. This would go on until someone got bored and said to his friend, "If I let you zap my picture, will you let me zap yours?" And this started a new game. One thing soon led to another, with little thought of any consequence. Then, one, perhaps called Bill, started squirting his friend, and they had a new game again. What really did the damage was Bill, who decided that the next time he got zapped he would disappear. He got zapped and vanished. Joe, not knowing that really no-one could get hurt, thought he had killed his friend."

"Overcome by remorse and regret, he ran off, weeping in his distress, not aware that the one he supposedly killed was over behind a cloud laughing his silly head off! The unfortunate result is simply that the one who killed, now, because of his conscience decides it is dangerous to zap anyone because he knows he mustn't kill. Therefore, he must reduce his power in case he does it again."

"So, you can see how this would no doubt multiply, and down Man would come. Now, you see Mankind on Earth, a very pale vestige of his true potential, locked inside his body, unaware of almost everything beyond his five senses. As he slides down the slope, Man, in losing his divinity, which allows his base side to dominate, becomes, in the extreme, brutish, crude, selfishly destructive, and blaming it all on something he created himself! The Devil!"

"But God, the Almighty, the Creator, the Power, the Wisdom, the Love, is not vindictive as base Man would have it. He has forever been quietly guiding, leading, and pointing Man to the day when he discovers himself, his true self, when he learns to use his Divine gifts, climbing painfully upward, learning important lessons as he climbs, and helping others as he goes."

"Then, after many trials and failures over many, many lives, at last, may he stand, fearful, humble, but proud. Then, perhaps, may the Almighty, All-powerful, All-loving Creator of All, reach out and say, Well done, thou good and faithful servant!"

For a time, Moira sat trying to grasp, to understand all the wondrous things they had been telling her. There was so much!

Her tutor gave his deep chuckle, "You have had quite enough for some little time! You are now going to take a nice long rest. After all, you have the whole of eternity to learn it all. And as I said, softly, softly."

He was right, of course. She needed to come up for air, to have a change. There was so much to see and do. So much in fact that she realised that it had been some time since she had a thought for Paul. She found it a pleasant surprise to see him again.

Paul Meets Sean

Paul looked at the figure before him, trying to make a quick and, he hoped, accurate assessment. He found too many surprises awaiting the unwary. But he saw a jolly face above broad shoulders, a stocky frame, and a hint of power; friendly towards him, he hoped.

"Yes," the man smiled, "Sean O'Leary, one-time priest, at your service." He sat down on the bench and invited Paul to join him. Paul slowly took the two paces to the bench and as slowly sat down. Perhaps it was the word priest that strengthened the trust he had begun to feel, but the general manner of the man helped a great deal. In reply to Paul's thought, he said, "As I said, I'm here to help and advise, and to tell you what you want to know. They," he pointed at the door, "They don't know I'm here. It wouldn't matter much if they did, for they can't hurt us. But it's best they don't know just yet. It would make things worse for you." Sean spoke in a rich Irish accent which felt very comforting, somehow. But he had to know who he was.

Sean answered, "Your friend, John asked me to come and see if you needed help. I am from one of the rescue teams we have here. You see, there are many who come here unexpectedly, like yourself. You were not ready for the transition, and we want to see if you can be brought to a higher state. We think you can. We already know a great deal about you, and we are sure that all you need is a few questions answered. Is that right?"

Paul thought a moment as he looked at Sean, who was not trying to be smart, condescending, or superior. He appeared to be nothing more than he said he was. Paul answered, "Well, yes, I suppose that's right. But how do you know about me? Can you read my mind or something?"

"Yes, we can, but don't worry," as Paul bridled at that, "For we don't need to. You will find we have a complete record of everything about everyone; you will find it can be a great help later." Paul, reluctantly, had to accept that for now. The relaxed friendliness of Sean helped. He went on, "I sure have a few questions! About all sorts of things. Such as how did you get in here? Where did you actually come from? Can you get me out of here? And my friend Jane?"

"Not so fast!" Sean held up his hand, "Not so fast! Yes, I can get you out, but we must do it so as to cause the least fuss, and of course, that includes your friend. As to how I got in here, that's easy when you know how. You will learn this is a realm of thought, and thought is all important here. I just picture myself in a place, and there I am."

"Well, can you just picture us out of here?" Paul was impatient, "I don't like this place, and I don't like Brother Elija!"

"Yes, yes, I will get you both out, I promise! But I want to see this Brother Elija first. We've heard a bit about him, and he will have to be stopped." Paul looked at him almost in awe.

Sean hastened to add, "No, don't you be getting any ideas about me! I'm just an ordinary man, nothing more." This, however, prompted Paul's next question.

"Why are you different from our friend Elija? You are both preachers or priests, aren't you? I mean, he's not to be trusted - I think! But you are like John, er, and Thomas too. So why the difference?"

Sean had a delightful chuckle, "Easy, me lad! It's all a matter of awareness. Awareness of self, not just the bits seen by mortal eyes."

He looked at Paul's raised eyebrows, "You know you are a spirit being?"

Paul nodded a little impatiently, "Yes, I know that! But is that all?"

"Dear me, no! That is just the first step you must take. And if I am to get you out of here in one piece, you will need to take a few more steps."

"Well, yes, fine, but what about this crazy man here? He has the whole place under his thumb?"

"You have nothing to fear from him, or anyone like him! This, I must teach you, and a lot more. So, are you willing to learn? Remember, I cannot help you unless you want it."

"If I have to learn to get out of here, let's get on with it. I sure want to know how to deal with guys like Elija. He used to burn witches, didn't he?"

"Yes, indeed he did, but so did we, much to my sorrow. My church committed terrible deeds, all in the name of Christ! I have yet to clean up that part for which I was responsible. But enough of that!"

"You said you were a priest. Is that right?" Paul demanded. Sean nodded with a wry grin, "Yes, I was, once. In fact, many times. And each time, I misused my position in not teaching the real truth. I taught the creeds and dogma of the church, but I did not teach what I now know to be true, although I suspected things were not quite as the book said. So, the first thing I want you to do is to forget all about the stuff you may have been told about death, heaven, hell, and the devil. Can you do that?"

"You mean all that stuff about Jesus is rubbish?"

"No, no! I don't mean that." Sean hastened to reply, "Much of what you've been told has been altered from the truth for various reasons. But the real teachings of Jesus stand in a very different light. They will take some little time to learn and understand, and much of that can come later. Do you want to go on?"

Suddenly a clang of the door being unbolted made Paul spin around, to see Jacob and his two heavies enter. Taking no notice whatever of Sean, they grabbed Paul, pinned his arms behind him, and bound his wrists. He struggled briefly, but they were too strong. He opened his mouth to call for help, but it would have done no good. Sean was nowhere to be seen. In desperation, he shouted, "Where are you taking me" He tried kicking out, but that earned a clout as they dragged him to the door. Jacob spoke up as they went, "Brother Elija wants to ask you a few questions, that's all! And you don't need to struggle! We're not going to hurt you."

"Then why tie my hands up like a criminal? I came here peacefully..." "Be quiet! You'll get a fair hearing! Elija is a just man." But Paul would not be quiet. "By what authority do you people set yourselves up as judges? You are Christians, aren't you?

"Be quiet, I said! Brother Elija..."

"Stuff Brother Elija! And stuff you too! Who do you think you are? I'm not a criminal!" Paul fought back.

He shouted, to delay being dragged before Elija again, he desperately looked about for Sean. He was nowhere to be seen. He looked at the small crowd that gathered to see what the fuss was about. They stared blankly back at him.

The guards quickly hustled him into Elija's court; Paul could not think of it in any other terms. Again, they had to await the judge's pleasure. And a good thing too, Paul realised. It gave him time to cool down. He would need as much clear thinking as he could muster. Of course, he had no idea of what was ahead, but he felt it wouldn't be pleasant.

Where had Sean gone, and how? He had started to hope things might be getting better, but now, disappearing just when he was needed - how in hell could these morons be stopped? A sinking feeling became stronger by the minute at Sean's continued absence.

Then, to his astonishment - and intense relief – a voice seemingly beside him whispered, "Courage, friend! I have not deserted you! All is well! There's nothing to fear! I'll take care of our friend!" There had been no words spoken, but he knew it was Sean, and the message was crystal clear. A reflex action made him look around the room. There were the guards whispering in a corner. Nothing else.

The big man strode in, scowling at Paul. He seemed annoyed at being dragged away from something. "Well?" Elija glared at Jacob, "What do you want me for? I'm rather busy just now, and I don't want to be disturbed." Paul's eyebrows shot up a few millimetres. So, Elija had not asked to see him! Why, then, was he here?

"Brother Elija," Jacob said obsequiously, "We think you ought to know that our prisoner is either possessed or mad. I thought it best if you tested him." There was an ugly undercurrent there that made Paul look sideways at Jacob.

"Botheration!" Elija sat down, scowling in displeasure, "Why couldn't it wait? I have other things to attend to." He fidgeted with a coat button. "Alright," he sighed heavily, "You had better tell me," and sat back expectantly.

Jacob cleared his throat, "I was listening at the prisoner's door, and I heard voices. So, I looked through the spyhole and saw him standing, looking at something and talking, but there was no-one there! So, I thought we'd better bring him to you."

Elija looked from Jacob to Paul, "Is this true? Were you talking to some-one?" Paul found himself answering, saying something he would never have thought of. He was saying, "Yes, brother, I was. I was praying to our God, the One True God. He answered and said he would send an angel to watch over me."

Elija sat a moment, slowly getting red. Then he exploded. "What blasphemy is this? How dare you lie to me! God speaks only to His chosen! You come here and claim to be such a one!"

Again, Paul found himself replying. "Brother, do you claim to have the sole right to God's words? Are you above mortal Man, to be chosen above others? Did not Jesus say, "Judge not, lest ye yourself be judged? Methinks, Brother Elija, you walk a very fine line" He found himself approaching the desk where Elija sat, frozen, with his jaw sagging. It seemed no-one had ever spoken to the good brother in such tones.

Paul turned slightly to show his bound wrists. "Me also thinks you had better release me from these bonds."

This was too much for Elija. He jumped up, screaming, "Take this...this..." and he suddenly fell silent, staring in shocked terror past Paul's shoulder.

"Who...who are you?" he whispered hoarsely, for standing beside Paul was a figure, shining with a blinding brilliance. The sudden appearance of Sean, dressed in flowing, glowing robes, was almost too much for Paul. The effect on Elija was devastating. The figure smiled at Elija, a soft, sorrowful smile.

"Why do you doubt my friend? Why do you treat him thus when he came to you in peace?" The figure moved slowly towards Elija, who hastily backed into the wall behind him. Paul recognised the cowardice of the bully.

Sean continued, "Methinks thou art a grievously troubled soul. Thou need urgent help."

"Who are you?" spluttered Elija, attempting to regain some poise, "How did you get in here?"

"I am a simple guardian of the just, and even of the unjust, should I be required. I am from the Heavenly Hierarchy, as you might say. Do you not know that you are on Heaven's doorstep?"

"Do you not know where you and your friends are?" Elija, seeing that Sean was not about to attack him, regained some of his bluster.

"This is Salem, in the state of Massachusetts. We are a God-fearing, devout community, permitting no ungodly behaviour." Paul caught a little grin from Sean as Elija said that, and wondered what he was up to. "Good Elija, this is not Salem in the United States of America. You are in an area close to what you would consider as Heaven. Do you know that you and your friends departed from life on Earth nearly two hundred years ago?" Elija had already drifted past the point where reasoning would reach him. He screamed for the two guards to capture the radiant figure before him, but the guards refused to move, too terrified of Sean. He stood, completely at ease, looking from one to the other. This was too much for Elija. He started towards

Sean but immediately thought better of it. He opened his mouth several times and clenched his fists. This had to be witchcraft! How could he possibly be dead? He was the same as he had always been.

The impossibility of it, along with Sean's appearance, was too much. He slumped to the floor, staring into space. Jacob stepped tentatively forward.

"Why have you come here? Are you really a messenger from Heaven?" "Gently, friend! I sense some alarm among you. I, like my friend here, come in peace. I came to help him, but I see I have a great deal to do here in this village of Salem."

"But you're dressed like a Roman Catholic priest! Are you one? Are you one of the Pope's terrible men? No good ever came from you! Leave us! Leave us! We want none of your popery."

"Ah, but I cannot do that! There are folk who are asking for help. As for being a Catholic, yes, I was one, before I came to this realm. Now I have learnt some of the real truth of life -and death- and I must pass that on to any who want it." He put his hand on Paul's shoulder. "This young man asked for help, and he shall have it. There are others here as well. But first, we must get help for Brother Elija. We will take him to our infirmary, where he will be able to cure his malady."

Jacob stepped forward to protest. "But. Why? There's nothing wrong with him."

"Yes, my friend, there is," Sean replied softly. "Elija is suffering from a sickness of the spirit and needs urgent help. He has been doing what he thought was right, but the sickness has turned him away from his true path."

As he finished speaking, two more shining figures appeared, one on either side of Elija. Smoothly, slowly, with Elija between them, they rose, soaring upwards and out the window, rapidly disappearing. Jacob and the guards fell to their knees, hands raised in supplication. Finally, Jacob found his tongue. "Where are they taking him?" he asked in an awed voice.

"To our hospital, where all disturbed arrivals go. He will be well cared for." Seeing the doubt in Jacob's face, he added, "You are wondering why we don't treat him as an enemy." Jacob looked blank, not willing to say anything to a man of obvious power. Sean smiled. "And you claim to be a Christian. Shame on you; his voice still gentle, he went on. "Have you no faith in what your master did not say. Succour, your enemies, did he not say. Love ye one another?" He chuckled; I see there are many things to talk about. Now..."

He turned to Paul. "As you see there's much to do here, if any of these good folk will accept our help. What I would like to do is set up a place where we could maybe talk to those who would listen. Of course, this cannot be forced in anyway. We can help only those who want it. I think you, and your good friend Jane could help a great deal. What do you say?

Paul, without realising his hands were free, held up his hand, "But, I can't teach!" Then seeing his hand as free, he stared at Sean. "Did you do this? How? I don't understand this, so how could I teach it?" While Sean had been talking, Paul became aware of the rustle of movement. He glanced at the door and saw, to his consternation, more guards entering. Sean turned as he finished speaking and looked with detached interest at the newcomers.

"We are arresting you for stealing our beloved leader and for blasphemy," It was Jacob who had taken a pompous, swaggering step forward, and drawing himself up to his full hundred and sixty centimetres, he roared, "Take them both!"

But the guards had other ideas. They flinched as Sean blazed forth. They managed a show of inching forward, but they stopped the moment Sean held up his hand. "Stay, friends! Come no further!" The men stopped as if running into a wall. "Your leader is gravely ill and needs urgent attention. No doubt, if he loves you as you love him, he will return to you when he is well again, and I promise you we can make him well."

"Witchcraft!" shouted Jacob as he tried to make the warding sign with his pudgy fingers, "In the name of the Holy Spirit, I order you to remove the...the thing you have used to stop us!"

Sean looked compassionately from one to the other. "Dear friends, I am from the Holy Spirit, and I am protected by the Holy Spirit. We know you don't understand, but if you will allow us, we can help you to learn."

"You see, we do not cringe before your invocation of the Power and love of Almighty God. We are all of God, all of us, everywhere. You cannot look anywhere and find a creation that is not of God! And did not God make man in His own image?"

"You say we use witchcraft! There is no witchcraft other than in the minds of ignorant, superstitious men, and there are no witches."

"You talk of the Devil, of Satan. There is no devil, no Satan, other than in the hearts of men, who would rather blame the devil for their misfortune than for not heeding common-sense actions taken for reasons of safety and well-being."

"What I have done, my appearance, and what you have seen

others do, all men can do. What I am, all men can be. That, and much, much more. What you do not know is that our own Jesus spoke thus many times to his men. I say it now to you."

"Once more, I tell you I come to help! I come in the Name of the Holy Spirit, to teach, to save, and to bring to understanding all those souls we can reach. I have to say these things at the risk of appearing a pompous fool."

"So, now we would like to gather all your people together to talk to them. Will you allow that?" Jacob looked from one to the other of the guards trying to read their faces. Three of them were decidedly unhappy. Sean said later they were very mixed in their ideas. They had been under Elija's bigotry for a very long time and had done some unpleasant things under his orders. If they now acknowledged him wrong, could they now blame him for their misdeeds?

Would that improve their chances? Should they be called to account? Although they had been following orders, they knew they were doing wrong. The fourth man was having none of it. He said as much as he headed for the door.

Paul added, "You lot bang your Bibles as much as you like. I'm off as soon as I find my girl!"

"I'm going too." It was Jacob, who went on, "I'm not having anything new at my age. I believe what I was taught, and it's sinful to listen to any heathen lies." He turned toward the door.

"Wait!" Sean held up his hand, "I think I can see your trouble. Listen." Jacob shrugged and stood, not really wanting to. "It's simply this." Sean touched him on the shoulder, to which Jacob flinched. "You lived on Earth about two hundred years ago. Is that right?"

Jacob bristled, "How could I? I'm not dead!"

"Yes, you are, and I can prove it to you, if you would like me to. Actually, you didn't die; only your body died. So, two hundred years later, don't you think we would have been able to carry on where the Bible stops? Remember, that was compiled from writings over two thousand years ago! All we have done is use Christianity as a starting place, as a basis for our knowledge, and gone on from there."

Sean knew very well he was taking some liberties in that statement, but it was a good way of overcoming solid bigotry until they could learn something of the real truth.

"No! No!" Jacob stormed, "You are telling me all lies! All lies! You would not dare talk like that before Brother Elija!"

Sean knew he was wasting his time, so he said, "Then goodbye, Brother Jacob. Our prayers and best wishes go with you. If you ever need help, just think of me."

"Never! Never! I do not talk to the Devil's men!" And he ran out the door for fear of any further contamination.

The remaining guards looked at each other, wondering if they were doing the right thing by staying. Then one spoke up, "For a long time, I have been looking at Elija. I think he's a bloody big fraud!" The man next to him guffawed, "Fraud? He's the biggest flamin' hypocrite you'll ever see! Do you know what the old bastard was doing when we brought the young'un in here" they all looked at him, waiting. "He was with his fancy piece! You know, the pretty dark girl, Mary. He spent as much time with her as he could, and a hell of a lot more than he should! And they weren't playing tiddly winks, either! Him keeping married couples apart! Ha!"

"You knew about that, Sean!" Paul looked almost accusingly at him. Sean grinned, "Yes, I did. I know many things and see much more! But it's not my place to judge or interfere unless there's a very good reason, as when someone's about to get hurt." He looked meaningfully at Paul. Then he turned to the others, "Right, then. Does my proposal meet with your approval? Shall we gather in your chapel? Remember, you are all free spirits. All I can do is lead."

The man who had spoken up first looked at the others, shrugged, and said, "I guess we got nothing to lose! I reckon we do that!" The others nodded, happy for someone else to make the decisions.

"Ok," he said, "I'll go and round them up. There's about forty here; most of them been trapped like you, and then kept!"

"Have they all been here since Elija came?"

"Oh, no! Some have been, only a few, really. Most of them just wandered in, like you did!" The men left, leaving Paul a little breathing-space to ask Sean one or two questions. The problem would be, he knew, that any time someone answers a question, it invariably raised more. The most pressing one right now was how did Sean appear and disappear seemingly at will?

"It's just a matter of vibration," he answered, "I'm no expert on physics; there are many more suitable to answer such questions. However, the way it was explained to me goes like this: "Every living thing is vibrating at a rate which is a result of several factors. The first would be the plane on which it lived. Whether plant, rock, water, fish, or fowl. All these things would be vibrating at the rate of that plane of existence. I see you are surprised at rocks being living things. Nevertheless, it's true."

"This vibration is peculiar to a particular plane. For instance, those trees over there," he pointed, "Would not be visible on the physical plane by anything while on that plane. You are aware you cannot see this plane while on the physical or earth-plane. And if we look at a plane higher than this, the same applies."

"You will also understand by now that not only is something visible, but it is also solid. On this plane, it is, because we also are on this plane. If we are just looking from another plane to this, for instance, we might see it, but not solidly. You understand?" Paul grimaced. "I think so!" he muttered.

"Now, that means," Sean continued, "that tree, that river, that ground, is fixed in location on the plane it occupies, for it cannot exist on another plane."

"But we, as we are actually Gods in the making, believe it or not, we have been given the priceless gift of mobility, and much, much more besides. Of course, not just physical mobility; we can create, we can perceive, depending on our individual level of development. Thus, we can choose what level of vibration we wish, so as to be where we want to be. We can also choose whether to be seen or not seen, and on which level."

"As we advance our development, so we can go where we want, and when desired can move out of sight, just by changing our vibration rate, and I can move to another plane, so long as that plane is within my tolerance, so to speak. For instance, I cannot go to the realm above my home realm, where your friend Moira is. I do not have the advancement for that as yet."

"Ah! I see now!" Paul grinned, "That's why we couldn't go there! I'm not sure I understand this vibration stuff, though. I remember someone raving on about it at college, only he called it oscillation, or frequency, or something…"

"Much the same," Sean nodded, "The way they told me about it was that all around us on Earth are all kinds of stuff - radio and television from transmitters all over the place. But we don't know they're there unless we have the right receiver to sort out only one of them - and only one! Otherwise, chaos."

"Now, although few know it, the Earth-plane is receiving vibrations, all of which are outside the range of human physical perception. These are the actual vibrations of this realm, and the ones higher and lower than this. All these are separated from the Earth-plane and from each other by their different rate of vibration. The higher the plane, the higher the vibration and the finer the texture".

"So, your entry to any of the higher realms is simply a matter of your own personal development. That is why you cannot, as yet, fully perceive the higher plane, let alone go there and feel comfortable."

He sat back, observing Paul to see how much of that had gone home. He seemed to have grasped it, but as they had come to expect, all this raised more questions. What, for instance, had actually happened, to arrive here after the crash?

"You arrived at the closest plane to the physical Earth, at the place where Thomas and John found you. Then you ran off blindly and found the tavern first; then you really headed off into the unknown! You went to the level just below this, where you met Billy and his boys. You will appreciate that they will be hard to reach with any meaningful help, though we have ways and means. And, of course, you didn't belong there, or you could not have left. Likewise, your friend Jane."

"The other lady, Eve, I think, went off with that other man; both OK, just don't see the need to change." Paul nodded dumbly, amazed at the accuracy of the account, but there was more....

Sean continued, "Then your friend Moira visited you. She lives in the realm just above this..." "Why?" Paul interrupted, "Is she better than me?"

"No, not really better," Sean gave his little grin, "Just slightly more advanced... Paul interrupted, "More advanced?" Sean grinned wryly, "Hell, I've got a degree! She hasn't!"

"No, my young friend, it's not that kind of advancement. I intend to show you if you are not so impatient. You then went to enter the level just above this, but your vibrations were not quite high enough to tolerate that. You see, it's not your actual worth, it's more your own estimation of yourself, and that is seldom wrong. You can visit a lower realm whenever you wish, because you are higher than that, and if you know enough about yourself, no harm could ever come to you there. Do you see now?"

Paul knew Sean was right in everything he had said; there was something about all this, something uncannily familiar; it was somehow a re-experience of something, somewhere, sometime. That was something else to catch up with. But he knew Sean was right, even if it was difficult to accept. It all made sense and pushing the déjà vu behind for the present, the rightness of it all gave him a composure and understanding new to him; he got a fleeting glimpse of how much he had changed.

Moreover, he knew how much he owed Sean for his easy friendliness, his account of the different realms, his non-judgemental understanding, and along with the over-riding certainty that he already knew all of this for the first time since the crash had precipitated him into this realm he felt a real confidence, an excitement even, about his future.

By the time they entered the little chapel, the guard who had spoken up before was telling them about Elija and Jacob. His name appeared to be Willis, and as he spoke was met by a wall of blank stares. Jane was there, and as she saw Paul, she hurried forward.

"Paul! Are you alright?" She grasped his arm, "They told me you were in for a hard time - I don't know why!" Paul patted her hand, "I'm fine! What about you?" Jane lifted her skirts to gasps of shock from the assembly and showed the bruises on her legs. She pointed to a beefy-looking woman. "She did this! And all because I said she was a fat cow!"

"She's a witch!" the woman screamed, "Look at her! No self-respecting lady dresses like that! And she ain't got no respect for decent folk! She don't even talk like us!" The dress part was true; she stood out like a flower among weeds. No, not quite right. Paul thought again; there were some mighty attractive women there, despite their drab clothing.

Sean mounted the little podium, bringing attention to himself for the first time. He had reduced his brilliance to a soft glow, but even that was enough to cause a few gasps and a cowering back among several of the women, including the fat cow.

"Good people of Salem!" Sean paused as he gazed around the assembly, causing a further flurry as his eyes met those few already terrified of him. "There is no need to fear me! I come in peace, in love, and in the name of Almighty God, who has sent me to you as a messenger, to bring you his love, and His promise of a richer life for you in this, the land of milk and honey."

"Your leader, Brother Elija, has been taken to the haven best suited to his many talents. And will no doubt return with much to teach you, and he will enlighten you with his new knowledge."

As he spoke, Sean demonstrated his skill at gaining the confidence of his audience through his sincerity of tone, his almost casual delivery, and by the aura of loving strength spreading throughout the little chapel. Even the fat cow was impressed.

He went on, "There are some aspects of your life here which seem long overdue for some explanation. As devout people, your lives are spent in toil, worship, obedience, and more toil. In reward for your belief, did He not promise eternal life? I have come to help you to understand what has been happening to you, where you are, and what to do to live full and rewarding lives in this; the beginning of your new life."

"Have you ever wondered why none of you have had any children here?" Gasps of shock and outrage from the few of Elija's original band made him smile and hold up his hands for silence. This was a little while in coming, for although there were only four of them, the noise was of many more. However, they were soon drowned out by the others who shouted things like, "We've had enough of bullying!" "Why don't you shut up!" "We'll send you off after Elija, you old cows!" and finally, Willis stepped forward. He bellowed, "Shut up! Shut up! Shut up! Listen! You might learn something," He had to repeat several times until, at last, there was almost silence. Sean nodded his thanks and went on,

"This is no time for fancy speaking!" He had their attention now, if not their agreement. He swept the gathering with his soft gaze, "I point out the fact that on Earth, men and women living together as man and wife usually have families. You do not. Is that correct?" Paul looked around at the puzzled frowns from those who could not grasp where Sean was leading. "I take it you agree." Nods, more, and whispers greeted that remark. "Here, you do not have children because," he held up a finger,

"One. You are not on Earth anymore!" A hubbub immediately burst out. Some nodded knowingly; some started shouting. Willis had to restore order again.

"And Two," Sean held up another finger, "There are no children because you now do not have your old bodies. These bodies you now have look exactly the same, but I assure you they are not. Nearly, but not quite the same."

"This is very easy to prove. Do you ever get hungry here? Can you drown in that river over there? Do you need to sleep? Where is the old day and night? Do you need to go to the lavatory?"

The four dissenters glared at him in fear and distrust, while a babble of anxious voices all talking at once tried to be heard. Paul caught snatches of, "I knew it! I've always known it!" Someone else was saying, "I've got to be dreaming! It's the funniest thing I've ever heard!" "What a load of rubbish!" from another. Finally, Willis bellowed, "Quiet!"

"Quiet yourself!" A man stepped forward, "You're one of Elija's men! Just a bloody turncoat! We'll get you too!" Willis stood his ground. "I had to, didn't I? I was always on your side! I had to keep my own skin whole!" Unabashed, he turned to the others, "Listen to this man! Can't you see he's telling the truth!"

This was met by abuse from the fat cow and her friends, while another group tried to shout them down. Sean stood, serene and calm, waiting for silence. The entire village had been suppressed for long enough; now, with the lid off, they were making up for it. Some were almost coming to blows in the heat generated.

Eventually, Sean ran out of patience. He, by a means remaining a mystery to lesser developed souls, raised his hands, and a clap of deafening thunder brought instant silence, with one or two dropping to their knees, hands raised in supplication. But now he could proceed.

"I didn't mean to startle you; I just needed quiet. Otherwise we get nowhere. I see what we must do! Those of you who would like to understand something of where you are and the life available to you, may come with us - my young friend and I."

"I can help any of you, but it must be your own choice, of your own free will. Any who would like that, please move over here!" He pointed to a spot close to him,

"Those who want to stay, go with them!" He pointed to the group rapidly moving away from them, looking fearfully over their shoulders, pursued by catcalls and not a little rude advice. Another clap of thunder allowed him to continue, "I can help those who want it. Those who already know it all and therefore cannot learn anything new can stay in your self-made prison."

"The freethinkers among you, come along with us. I can promise that you'll be well cared for until you wish to fend for yourselves." In the surge of bodies all moving in their chosen direction, one young girl took a mighty swipe at the fat cow as she passed. "That's for the nasty bitch you are and for all the things you've done to us!" The fat cow staggered back, screaming. "Heathen! I always knew…"

"Silence!" Sean roared in exasperation. "You're lucky I don't turn them loose on you. But then, if you were real Christians, they wouldn't hate you like this. But I fear you are only pretending. But we're wasting time with you bigots."

He turned to the others, looking up at him almost in awe. He had to put a stop to this, so he grinned and pointed to the door. "Last one outside's a dirty rascal!" In a rush, they quickly gathered outside, the rear-guard glowering at them.

Willis promoted himself to sergeant of the little band and for no other reason than he thought he should, made a headcount. There were thirty-two ready to move out with Sean, and with no reason not to, he led them quickly across the little bridge to freedom.

They had gone only a short distance when Paul looked back. There was nothing there - no bridge, no village. Surely, they hadn't come so far already? He stood, slightly bemused a moment, then shrugged and followed the others. Just another unexpected side to this bewildering place. They reached a pleasant little glade at which Sean called a halt. He knew all were bursting with questions such as what was in store for them, who is this man who makes thunder by clapping his hands, and why did they feel he was worth trusting?

He sat them down in a semi-circle, beamed at them, and very quickly had them at ease. He told them all the things that were usually little more than dreams, flights of fancy of mere mortals. Keeping it simple and basic, he told them about themselves, what had happened to them, where they were, and why. He told them how this realm was a realm of thought and that each one of them was a result of their own thoughts, and this governed their appearance, their surroundings, and their attitude to others.

"Very largely," he went on, "Your thinking is monitored, even controlled by what you consider is correct, acceptable to others, and by what others will allow. Elija was insistent about what you were allowed; he told you what to think. He would not let anyone think for themselves."

"Therefore, very little of the real truth ever got through to you, and because of that, there has been no personal development at all. Here, we encourage each one who comes here to expand their knowledge, their own beingness as it were."

"There is no compulsion in this; you are all free beings and must always make your own decisions. We help, and that is all we can do. Remember, none of you are much different from what you were on Earth. Therefore, your surroundings here are just what you are able to accept within your own experience."

"The real key to life here, is in the realm of Soul, where it is your own awareness of your spirituality, your divine origin, and your true potential to expand into the cosmos."

"This is merely the precis of God's teaching. What occurred was much more exciting". Sean actually said very little; instead, he projected onto the receptive minds of his audience illustrative scenes of them leaving their bodies behind at the body-death, the basic being appearing in this realm. He showed the potential of their new existence, the natural divisions of the cosmos, and where each of them fitted.

Then he took them on a pictorial tour of the real nature of Planet Earth, as part of the Solar body, how the entire solar system is a huge entity in its own right and is indissoluble as part of the whole. He showed them the elementals, the nature spirits, the Deities, and angels all working with the Earth Goddess, the living entity which is Earth, and how mankind's continued greed and arrogance were destroying the delicate system maintaining the four basic elements, earth, air, fire, and water in close harmony.

Finally, he showed them the different planes of thought, which always portrayed the state of a person in terms of experience and attitude, thus placing them on that plane. He showed them how each plane related, in higher vibrations, to the next higher - or lower - vibration, similar to the different stations on a radio band; each one different in frequency, and that one's place on any of these was according to their awareness and development.

Paul was, at last, able to understand why he was unable to do other than look briefly at the realm next to this, where he believed Moira to be. Further, he had to stop thinking of the realms as being either above or below. Sean covered that point; he showed them there was neither up nor down, simply a shift in perception, of awareness. As numerous radio emanations are present constantly, all impinging on the same spot, so it was with these realms of existence. At last, some of the mystery was revealed!

As Sean went on to describe how one must balance the books, to correct a wrong done, or to do something one had left undone, before any progress could be made, a little more of the picture fell into place.

"Of course," Sean gave his little laugh, "You can stay on one level, in one realm, for as long as you like. There is plenty of things to do if you look for them. Here is where you use your very precious power of choice."

Paul lost track of what Sean said after that. He was much too busy trying to find something he had done or not done, for he was determined to find his way to the realm where Moira was. He tried to look down on his life, and saw one or two things which made him shy away rather quickly. These, he was definitely not ready to face. He found a couple that he could handle, he thought. The deep ones were another matter. There was a deep shame there and not a little pain. Later he learned how to cope with memories such as that, but not yet! Definitely not yet!

He could face the time he put a dent in the boss's car as he tried to park his own. He never admitted it; he thought he might lose his job. Then there was the time when he had left his friend to get caught during a student hi-jinks. It was the usual rowdy prank during capping. Although none of his mob were to be capped, they all joined in the fun. They had been attempting to steal the wheels off the Mayoral limousine when they were spotted. Three of them fled, leaving the fourth, trapped behind a door, to be caught.

Paul had unthinkingly closed it cutting off the last man's escape. The police had charged him with breaking and entering, and attempted burglary. The mayor himself came to the rescue, and after some argument, he persuaded the police to drop the charges. For quite a while after that, Paul had justified his desertion of his mate, believing he would have stepped forward if the mayor had not. He firmly believed he would have shared the blame. Snow. Snow White, that was him. "Hey! Wait a minute!"

He sat upright with a jerk. He remembered about him. Snow White was here! Somewhere. He had wiped himself off by running into a concrete wall on his motorbike. Paul had attended his funeral. Fancy forgetting that! As soon as Sean was free, Paul asked him how he could find out about Snow, and if he could go to where he was.

"Easy!" Sean grinned, "Just picture him, as you remember him, and you will go there, if he is on this plane, or a lower one, no matter. But before you go dashing off! I've a feeling you need to square something with him. Tell me about it, and I can advise you, maybe."

Paul soon told it all. Sean gave his little chortle, "This is going to work out beautifully! Your friend is on the same plane - vibration-wise - to this, where you met your friend Billy. At Paul's gasp of astonishment, he went on, "Oh, ho, me lad, don't be so surprised! I saw your picture of him, then sent out a scout or two, and they found him among thieves and layabouts."

"All in a moment? How can you work so fast?" "The experts tell me this time stuff is purely subjective. It exists only by your considering it. The point is, you can go and bring him back - if he wants to be rescued, that is. If you do, you will have settled your account and learnt a great deal in so doing. A wonderful chance for you. With what you know and a few little wrinkles I can give, there will be nothing and nobody that can hurt you in that place. What do you say?"

Paul was on the spot. If he agreed, went, and failed, then what? If he refused, was he no more than a windbag?

"I'll show you something that will help you." Sean stood up and pointed to a tree about twenty metres away. "Now, I want you to go over to that tree!" Paul took a step, puzzled at the request.

"No, not like that!" Sean stopped him, "Just get a picture of yourself standing beside it. Off you go!" Almost before he had finished speaking, Paul was there, looking back with something approaching terror.

"How...how..." he spluttered. "Remember, I said that this is a world of thought? All thoughts are much more meaningful than where you lived. There, thoughts are masked by the gross nature of heavy matter. The most important factor, there, here, or anywhere in the cosmos, is a thing called certainty. If you have a thought, say, that you can walk on that water over there - and no other thought! - you will do just that. But when you start by saying 'I can walk on water' then as you get close to it, you wonder if you really can do it, saying 'Don't be stupid! Of course, I can't walk on water!' So, you step out, and in you go. From then on, you know you can't walk on water."

"So, positive thoughts only! No negative ones. Just now, you had no time to get negative. Now, come back here! At once! Now! Come!" The peremptory command left no room for anything but instant obedience, and once more, he stood beside Sean.

Elated and still slightly terrified, he let out a huge whoosh of breath. "Is that how you disappeared when they came for me in their bloody gaol! Whee! It's a bit scary, though! Suppose..." He was thinking about what happens if you get stuck halfway!

"Suppose nothing, me boy! Back on Earth, this works just the same, only usually you would be leaving your heavy carcase behind, and of course, to become separated from that is an immediate expectation of body death. Can be upsetting to the unwary, and that, of course, goes for almost everyone back there. Here, you don't have that problem; you have the body you have created yourself, your spiritual body, or more correctly, bodies. You will find out about that later."

"But why is this not known back in the physical world? I feel someone's been keeping people ignorant. Does anyone know about this back there?"

"Oh, yes, quite a few," Sean grimaced ruefully, "And I - and a lot more like me - as one who used my bigotry - and authority as a priest - to squash such things. It was my task to persecute those I could. I'm ashamed to admit that the Church - no, all churches - have a great deal to answer for. Many terrible things were done in the name of our church, and each and every deed must be paid for in full by us all. In fact, I have to start the repayment very soon now, and the proper place to do that is where the evils were done, on our own Earth. I must return."

"But how can you do that? Will you be a ghost? Haunt people?"

"Oh, no!" Sean laughed, "Nothing like that! Mind you; there are a few earth-bound souls who stay around a place after their death to terrify those that see them and are so-called ghosts. Oh, yes, they're real, alright. No, what I must do is to be re-born into a body so as to live the kind of life whereby I might be able to undo some of the wrongs I've done."

"So, reincarnation is not a load of rubbish! It's true then!"

"Yes, my lad, it's true! It's the best way to learn, and to right any wrongs and balance your own personal accounts."

"But didn't you say a while ago that we are free, and nobody can tell us what to do?"

"Yes, indeed! That is correct. But I choose to go. I don't have to - but if I wish to develop and advance myself, I must. It's up to me entirely."

Paul stood, looking at the jocular face before him. This was a man who confessed to having been a priest in a hierarchy renowned for its stern, unbending views, now talking in terms more in keeping with the ones who had traditionally been targets of the same hierarchy! What would have caused such a change of view, a U-turn of such magnitude?

Sean gave a rueful little laugh, "One is forced, by sheer weight of evidence, to open one's eyes and to accept those things outside of Creed and Dogma, and which show how incredibly narrow are the same creeds and dogma. We, or more particularly, I, had learned the true teachings of the Great Master Jesus, and these teachings are enormously broader, more encompassing than any of us ever realised."

"These teachings are available to all, even to Brother Elija, who is suffering from the same complaint as myself on first arriving here. He and I believed what we had been taught, but both of us had been taught from erroneous sources..."

"Yes, I see that," Paul interrupted with a frown, "But how do I get on? How do I, in my ignorance, accept what you say, when I might just as well accept what Elija says? What reason can I have for believing anyone? There seem to be so many different ideas and bloody doctrines - who is right? How in hell can I tell?"

"There you are, me boy," Sean muttered to himself, "Talk your way out of that!" He sauntered over to Paul, "You sure know all the awkward ones! Let's see now...about all, I can give you right now is a bit of general background, and you might see where the trend is."

Paul shrugged, "Everything you've said so far makes a bit of sense, in a way. So, I'm listening."

"Have you ever wondered why there are so many little branches within Christianity? Ah, I see you have. And you also know something about the intolerance between, say, the Jehovah's Witnesses and, say, the Brethren, or the Latter-Day-Saints."

"Always banging on the door!" Paul snorted, "With their own brand of salvation!"

"Yes, but also don't forget the ones that don't bang on your door. The main churches, all of them, are just as divided, even among themselves." Sean continued, "The point is, they all miss the point. It's as if there is a huge mural, say, on a wall. The entire truth about God, mankind, life, death, and so on, is displayed there for all to see. But what usually happens is that one man is attracted to a part of the picture, and to get a better view, he moves closer to it. But when he does that, he loses the view of the whole. He becomes taken by the small truth he has seen, and with a little wild imagining, believes he is seeing the total. Of course, he is not. But he now goes forth spreading his little morsel of truth, believing it to be all. Now comes the trouble, for someone else has done the same thing, and another, and another, until each has seen a portion of the whole -correct in itself - but he cannot accept that what another has seen is also correct."

"The result is as you know it; Each one of these 'prophets' has seen what the others have not, and each one claims he saw the truth. None have seen the entire mural. So, while each one is right as far as he goes, none have seen the totality of it. Now, you are immeasurably ahead of most, for you know they cannot see how limited they are, and if they don't know their knowledge is limited, they will never accept any new knowledge."

"You, my friend, can now go forth and obtain the knowledge you seek because you realise how much you do not know, and you've already started on that road. Now, does that help?"

Paul pondered a moment and decided it did help, but once again, it raised more questions. For example, what does the entire mural look like? Sean lay back his head and roared with laughter, while Paul stood scowling, nonplussed and embarrassed. At last, Sean wiped his eyes, shook his head, almost laughed again, but regained control as he saw Paul's discomfort. At last, he spluttered, "Sorry! Oh, sorry! Please forgive an old man! But you don't realise what you said!"

Paul glared at him. "Alright! Alright! What did I say that's so bloody funny?" Serious again, Sean placed his hand on Paul's shoulder, "My dear boy, finding out what's on that mural will take up your entire existence. Even for those who continually seek the truth, they're at it virtually forever, even in our terms."

"But many don't want to know, and that's their privilege. They can stay happily in one place until they get bored stiff a few hundred years or so, physical universe time. Then if they decide they want to learn and develop, away they go to the advanced schools available, or to a reincarnation or two or three to learn a bit more, or of course, to re-pay a karmic debt or two. Make up your own mind as to what you want; it's your choice. You can go as fast – or as slow - as you want, or you can just stand still if you can stand it. But as I see you, you're one of the ones who need to know the answers, and standing still is not for you. So - first, go and find your old friend and see what you can do for him."

As Sean finished speaking, a figure appeared between them. It was Moira, looking very beautiful, dressed in a lovely flowing creation in smoky blue, setting off her complexion perfectly.

"Hullo Paul! I thought it was about time I paid you a visit. You're looking good!"

Paul stood, completely taken aback by her sudden appearance, coupled with her obvious pleasure at seeing him. Their last encounter had not been so friendly! All he could do was mutter, "Moira! What a surprise! What brings you to want to see me?"

"Oh, I needed a little break, so I decided to see how you're getting' on."

"Thanks to my friend Sean here," Paul nodded to Sean as he spoke, "I'm doing better than I thought I would! He saved me - and these others - from a spot of bother, and "has taught me a lot!"

"Only what you asked for, Paul!" Sean beamed, "You entertain your friend while I go and talk to the others."

He left them together, looking at each other, Paul feeling slightly embarrassed. Moira understood his diffidence, for she had been quite cool. Now she seemed warm and friendly. She could sense his uncertainty, for she said, "We've both changed since that night!" She gave a little laugh, "I've learned a lot, and I can see, so have you. I knew that if you had the chance, the real you would come out. It has started to!" Paul looked at her blankly. She had always been more the opposite, reluctant to express herself openly. Now, perhaps because of the close interchange of thought being the norm of which almost all on this lower level were quite unaware, he looked at her with renewed interest. He had never been quite sure what had attracted him in the first place; it wasn't sex because she kept to herself and was definitely not available.

Perhaps it was that her unattainability had attracted him or her innate gentleness, her kindness to others. He had never given it much thought, other than she was regarded as the catch of the season.

Now, she was alive and vibrant, much more extroverted. Most importantly, she appeared to have forgiven him for being responsible for her sudden transition from Earth to Astral. However, he was still not sure.

He had asked, "What brings you here?" Her immediate reply was, "Why, to see you, of course! My, but you have changed" He stood looking at her, puzzled. He hadn't changed; she had. He said as much, which brought a peal of silvery laughter. "Not changed? Dear Paul, don't you know you've become a human being? I'm very proud of you, in fact."

Paul frowned and shook his head slightly, "I don't know what you mean! I've done nothing other than just managed to keep out of trouble, that's all!"

Sean interrupted his little talk to his group to saunter over to them, laughing as he came, "That's what you think, me boy! If it hadn't been for you, we would never have run into our friends here, and Elija would still be here with his personal brand of bigotry. You alerted us to a job that needed doing!" and he went back to his attentive audience.

"So just settle down and just be yourself again, and you might be surprised." Moira took his arm in a gesture of friendship as he tried to understand their attitude.

"Hell, he had done nothing!" You put out an unconscious plea for help when they put you in their prison, and those in the rescue teams hear such things. Sean heard your call and came. So, you get the credit, so to speak. Now, what else have you been up to?" Paul had to accept what they said, but he had to note that this was probably the first time anyone had praised him for helping anyone else. "Oh," he said off-handly, "Just been trying to find a way to get to Emerald City - you know, where you are."

"Emerald City! That's nice! What made you think of that?"

"Oh," He was suddenly embarrassed, "You know - the land of Oz, Yellow Brick Road, the Wizard, and all that rubbish."

"What a lovely idea! What made you think of that?"

"Forget it, will you!" Paul said almost roughly, "It's nothing. But, what's it like there? I've been trying to go there, but I can't."

"You will soon, I'm sure! What's this little expedition you're going on?" You might be surprised at what comes out of that."

"You mean, I might be rewarded?" he asked sceptically. "No, from what I understand, it doesn't work like that. It's your attitude, more than anything else, that changes. And as I'm sure your friend Sean has said, that is a measure of your own personal development."

"Yes, I understand that," Paul said impatiently, "What's it like there? What do you do with yourself?"

"Oh, all sorts of things. We can go to concerts, drama, opera. There are schools, libraries, universities; I've even found out there are research laboratories. There's animal refuges..."

"Animal refuges? What do you mean?"

"Of course, this would be new to you. I got a big surprise myself when I met up with my two Siamese cats. You remember them? Well, they were both waiting for me! I was overcome!" She lapsed into silence as she fondly recalled it.

"Cats!" Paul said eagerly, "Cats! Does that mean dogs too? Maybe I'll find Boney there! Do you think I could?"

Moira laughed. "Most likely, I should say. Boney, that's a funny name!" "Oh, it's supposed to be Ebony, but I couldn't say that when I was small. So, it became Boney. He was a black Labrador."

Moira kept him busy asking endless questions for what seemed like forever. Eventually, he wound down, and she was able to draw his attention to a girl standing, looking at them, a wistful expression on her attractive face. Paul glanced at her, and, seeing it was Jane, hurriedly looked away. Moira knew something was up and said quietly and uncritically, "Come on, Paul! There's no secrets here, and no silly jealousies! Who is she?"

"Just...just someone I met out in the wilds..." "But she's a friend, isn't she?" Moira astonished him by her friendly, easy tones, "Why don't you ask her over? I'd like to meet her!"

There was none of the competitive, even spiteful attitudes of old Earth; no misplaced ideas of ownership, of that almost indecent passion generated by two people who 'belong' to each other.

Jane, however, was diffident at answering Moira's beckoning wave. She had yet a little distance to go to reach Moira's easy manner. "Who," she thought, "Is the sweet-looking bitch sitting so close to my Paul?" He finally persuaded her when he said, "Please, Jane! Come and meet an old friend of mine!" Jane looked from one to the other and was met by nothing but easy, relaxed friendliness and slowly came over to them.

Paul sprang to his feet and, taking her by the hand, introduced her. In no time, she was seated between them, and spent some time chatting with them. After that pleasant interlude, Moira stood up and declared she had to leave them, for there was an important lecture she didn't want to miss. She gave both Paul and Jane a little peck on the cheek and said, "Good luck on your little jaunt, and I'll see you both before very long. 'Bye for now!" And she was gone.

Paul and Jane sat almost in a dream-like state after she had gone. Her presence had been a great help, but it had done nothing to dispel the unreality of their experiences. People appearing, then disappearing, thoughts being as clear as speech, and the almost unbelievable just-witnessed change from sexual- driven relationships to affiliations based on much more durable values.

One conclusion reached almost simultaneously by them was that this was because here, in these realms, concealed thoughts and motives were not possible. Lower, in the less refined realms, yes, things could be hidden to some degree, simply because nobody there could easily accept thoughts as being seen by others, even if it were happening before them. Further, in their ignorance, they completely discounted any such thing during their earthly existence, when occasionally it does occur!

"Do you still love her, Paul?" It was Jane, breaking the mood, returning him to the present. "I...I don't know," he answered uncertainly, "I think I did, but she's changed somehow; got more friendly and easy to talk to, but more - I dunno – harder to get, if you know what I mean. She's...a lot more open and nicer than before, but something else is different, and I don't know what!"

Sean came over and sat beside them, and as usual, Paul had his questions at the ready. "You said, back there somewhere, that people don't change because they leave their dead bodies behind and come here. That's right, isn't it?"

Sean nodded, "That's right. What's the problem?" "Moira, my friend who was just here, has changed from being almost a haughty little madam, to a friendly uncritical person. Uncritical she was not! Easy and relaxed also, she was not. Now she is. Why?"

"It's a matter of innate awareness on first arrival. Usually, then, for those with little or no awareness of self or what might have happened, they graduate to the level most suited to their character and the regard - or lack of it - in which they hold others. These ones usually do not change, certainly not easily. Now, when someone like Moira arrives, she, at first, displayed all the attitudes which were basic to her background, as you did yourself.

But any who have minds sufficiently open and receptive to new ideas can take advantage of what is offered by many, such as myself. You have done so, and of course, Moira. Remember, all one needs to admit is that he doesn't know. He can be taught. I would like to quote to you a very ancient saying I picked up during my last incarnation in India. This says it all:

"He who knows, and knows not that he knows, is asleep – wake him.

He who knows not, and knows he knows not, is a child – teach him.

He who knows not, and knows not that he knows not, is a fool – shun him.

He who knows, and knows that he knows, is a wise man – follow him."

He stood, raised his hand to forestall Paul already with his mouth open, "I am in the second of these categories. I am very much a child and am very busy learning." And he turned and walked off, leaving them to make whatever they could of that. At first, Paul could make very little. For all his broadening views and more enlightened outlook, he was not over-impressed by sonorous philosophies. But then, he had not reached the stage of being able to differentiate high-sounding but largely empty phrases, from the real truth. However, he was able to agree with Sean in that he knew nothing, and wanted to learn, and that the whole quotation was concise, even beautiful.

At last, he stood and, helping Jane to her feet, said, "I guess I'd better get doing something instead of just loafing around!"

"What are you going to do, then?" Jane asked with a little frown.

"Oh, I want to go and find an old friend who's been here for just about a year now. He was killed when he hit a brick wall riding his motorbike. Sean said he's somewhere in the area where I met you."

"Oh, you can't go back there!" Jane replied, a little afraid, "You know what it's like! They'll kill you!" Paul laughed, but there was a little thread of uncertainty there, "They can't hurt me! Or so Sean said! So, I'll be alright!"

"Then I'm coming with you! I'm not going to lose you now!" She clutched his arm, "You remind me of my kid brother, and we were very close. He died of some fever when he was only fourteen, I think." A sudden thought flicked across her mind. Could it be possible? Could Paul be that brother? Paul understood simultaneously, paused, and shook his head,

"I dunno, do I? I can't remember ever living before. I was born in Wellington on August the tenth, nineteen sixty-five, and I don't know of anything before that. Yeah, I know Sean goes on about living before, but I can't see it. What for, anyhow?" he turned and faced her, "And you can't come with me, anyway. I must do this on my own, and it will be better because I would be worrying about you all the time. And I probably won't be very long." He gave a little snort, "And you said I might get killed! How can I? I'm already dead!" he finished with a loud guffaw.

Jane attacked him in annoyance, "It's not funny! They might do, oh, all sorts of things…"

"No way!" He was positive, "I have the means to escape any time I want, and no-one can hurt me!" And although he said it and meant it, there was a tiny seed of doubt. He knew Sean would be able to cope in any situation, but could he?

One way to overcome that little niggle, he thought, would be to get in a little practice. So, he went on a tour of all the places where he had been; the tavern, the cottage, now occupied by some strangers, back to the tavern, and then after that, he felt bold enough to visit the lair of Billy the butcher. He appeared there, ready to flee, but the place was deserted. There were signs of occupation, but he could not tell by just looking how fresh - or old - the signs were.

Feeling quite pleased with himself, he went back to the glade, where the escapees - or were they refugees? -from Elija's compound were still under instruction from Sean. He was telling them about their ethereal bodies and why they seemed so solid. "It's a matter of where you are," He told them, "Our scientist friends tell me that back on the Earth-plane that everything, including bodies, trees, rocks, water, even air, are made up of millions of tiny particles with relatively huge gaps between. If you went there now, as you are right now, you would pass right through any of that as if it were just smoke. Here, it's just the same, only on a different level."

"On earth," he continued, "you thought you were solid; here, you still think of yourselves as just as solid. Indeed, you are, from your point of view. And that is the key to it all. I am here, and you are here, and we all agree on that. And the spread of agreement - how widespread it is - gives us our reality on any subject you fancy."

"We are here simply because we say we are, and we, and our surroundings, are just as solid as we say they are. This is because we are now in the realms where thought is all. Everything you see here is the result of someone thinking it is so, and it becomes as solid as agreement grows concerning that thought."

After a short while, to give his audience time to digest what he had said, he stood and raised his hand for their attention. "As you can see, there is little here to make us want to stay. We have no buildings and nothing else, really. While we could provide them as we might wish, it will probably be better if I take you to a place that already exists. You need a pleasant stable place where you would be welcome."

"I propose, therefore, to take you to a little village where there will be room for all, if you wish to make it your new home. The folk there are the same as yourselves, and they have all accepted our basic help to understand more about themselves. Those who would like that, please move over to this side." He pointed, "And we shall see how many want to go along."

Paul was not really surprised when all of them moved. They had been willing enough to follow Sean away from Elija's compound and were all adventurous enough for more. What he was curious about was how to move thirty-two people. Sean caught the drift of the thought and chuckled. "He! He! Simple! We walk! It's not far." Paul was mystified now, for they set off along the path he and Jane had come along. He was certain it was the same path, but he could not remember any village in this area.

Further, their surroundings became more like a luminous tunnel than a path through woodland. Little was discernible on either side or even ahead. Then, without warning, they were there. Or so they had to understand, for suddenly they were in a village square, surrounded by neat cottages complete with gardens. Quite a few people saw them arrive, and they were surprised to see the welcoming smiles and gestures as they met and quickly mingled. Then a cry of recognition went up as a woman clasped a newcomer to her bosom.

"Sarah! My sister! Oh, Sarah" The rest was muffled by their tears of joy, and Paul found an unexpected lump in his throat, giving further wonder at the similarity of bodies, physical and etheric. Both responded alike to emotional situations. Cottages were quickly found for the newcomers, much to their surprise. They just seemed to appear among the trees, but Paul was still not accustomed to the absence of any time references. There was no night or day, no clocks, no sun moving across the sky. So, what seemed like 'at once' could quite possibly be any time interval. He was starting to realise that this was the most difficult concept to understand in the realms of spiritual existence.

What was pleasing, however, was the complete lack of nonsense about gender here, as different from that in Elija's stronghold. Here, people paired off as they wished, and it mattered not a whit of difference what their original relationship may have been. There were family groups who wanted to maintain the bond, but there were also those who had no desire to continue a past relationship. And were quite free to do as they pleased with no rancour or jealousies. This was brought about by the easy sharing of thoughts, which made it difficult to be false or hypocritical in this atmosphere. As Sean had pointed out, this was the realm where most reasonably minded ones would gravitate. Those not stuck in any doctrine- or lack of. Any of the ones who were receptive to new ideas, or at least willing to look, came here.

To these basically honest people, such open attitudes were beautiful to behold, and they enjoyed the almost idyllic life in the village. Paul realised he was procrastinating in starting out on his quest. Who knows what he might run into, and would he really be able to handle what may come his way? The more he thought about it, the less attractive it became.

Another powerful excuse for the delay was Jane. From a flashy tart, a whore; in the time he had known her, she had become a sensitive, intelligent, and delightful companion. He was at a loss to understand the change, but she was able to clear it up.

"Do you remember when we tried to enter that place? The one where…" "Yes, I remember!" Paul grimaced; he had never been so helpless, so wrong-footed ever before.

"Me too," Jane agreed, "but it was then that I changed. Do you remember what I was like? I'm sure you didn't think much of me." "Well…" "Don't try to pretend you didn't." There was no malice or bitterness: she kissed him, stroking his cheek, smiling, looking at him as she spoke, "because you were right. I was just a little tramp, a prostitute, of no intellect or sense of values. All I knew was how to get a living out of men."

"But that little glimpse we had of that place brought it all back. My previous lives brought up why I was just a tart. You see, I had been quite the lady, back at the end of the eighteenth century. I was the wife of a rich Londoner, although it was only wife in name. He was a womaniser, had a new girl almost every week."

"Then he got one he set up in an apartment where he would go to see her. I found out about her and had her beaten and disfigured. She never had another man after that. But I didn't know that I would have to pay for that. I was, of course, completely unaware of her circumstances and that she did what she did in order to live. The fact that my husband chose her made her my enemy, when the real enemy was my husband, and I don't want to know where he is, either. He got killed in the war. He's nothing but a stinker. Anyway, because I ruined a life, I had to pay, which I did. I had to become a prostitute to learn about poverty and hardship, and now, of course, I understand what drives young girls to it. About the only thing I don't quite understand is why men are always chasing girls, and only for one thing. Do you know why?"

Paul looked askance at that. He was a male, virile, and were not females' fair game? You scored wherever and whenever you could, didn't you? "Oh, you men!" Jane scolded. "You go about begetting children all over the place with never a thought for the mother of the child!"

"Hang on there!" Paul objected, "We're not all like that! Oh, I suppose a few..." "A few!" Jane scoffed, "A few! Do you know how many prostitutes there are in London? Paris? New York? No, I don't know either, but any girl who's any good gets a good living, all because men want what they've got!"

Paul knew he wasn't going to win that argument, so using that as a spur - how many times has a man dashed off to battle because he lost an argument with his female companion? - He decided he would gird up his loins and go forth.

"Well, OK, you win! I'm off to find my friend, Snow. I don't know how long it will take; maybe no time at all!" He kissed her and went off to find Sean. He had gone no-one knew where. "Hm!" he snorted, "Going off without saying..."

"What's up?" and Sean stood beside him, "I'm only a thought away, you know. No need to say goodbye here!" "Yeah, well," Paul tried to shrug off the discomfort of his empty complaint, "I'm off now, to find my friend, Snow. What do I do?" "Just whatever you need to do! Just remember what I told you before; no-one can hurt you unless you let them. Off you go then, and good luck!"

The Search

The dismal little glade was much the same as it had been on Paul's last visit. He had come direct, by the now easy method of just forming a picture in his mind of where he wanted to go, and there he was. Just as simple.

He appeared before the crude shelter to find a group of unsavoury characters huddled in a knot. A girl saw him first and screamed at him, at which the three men in the group sprang to their feet, advancing menacingly. And they were big. But he had his ace whenever he needed it. He held up his hand.

"I come in peace! I am neither thief nor villain. I am looking for a friend, and you might be able to help" The advancing trio paused as they saw he was unarmed.

"Alright, pretty boy! Come any closer, and I'll brain you!" Trembling inside but determined to bluff it through, he raised his arms, "I'm not coming any closer, never fear! All I want is some information. Can you tell me if there is a town or village in these parts?"

The one who had threatened him growled, "Can you pay?" Paul scoffed, "There's no money here!" hoping they had never seen any, but of course, he was wrong.

"Oh, yes there is!" The man rummaged around in his pockets and produced a few coins. "What's this! Money, that's what! Like I say, no money, no information! You get nothin' for nothin' here." But it turned out that Paul needed none. Having spent some time with a few souls who knew a few things, his own latent abilities had been stimulated into activity, and as Sean had told him on numerous occasions, it was all a matter of awareness. These folk were knowledgeable of little beyond their old Earth-bound limits and were totally unaware that they were telling him what he wanted to know, of a settlement not too far from here.

It was more a fortress than a village and seemed to be ruled by another despot. There seemed to be quite an infestation of such types here!

Paul recalled what Sean had said on another occasion, that these types were criminals on Earth, and upon arrival here, discovered that there were no law-keeping police or sheriffs, very soon gravitated by threat, treachery, and plain villainy to a position of power and authority.

In a small way, that was Billy, the bully. Give him time, and he would be the boss of a larger outfit. And, of course, Brother Elija, masquerading under a religious banner but nonetheless still a despot. The picture he was now getting of this leader was true to form, and he knew he would have to be careful.

However, now having the information he required, he replied, "Sorry to have troubled you. I don't have any money; we don't use it where I come from. I'll go on my way." He turned to go when the big man shouted, "Hey! Hang on! What do you mean, you don't need any?"

Paul looked over his shoulder as he spoke, "Money's no good if you can't spend it. Are there any stores around here? I've not seen any."

"Yeah, well..." the man hesitated, "I had to go some to get this! I ain't got nothin' without a bit o' brass in my pocket!"

Paul could detect an undercurrent of robbery with considerable violence as the man unwittingly pictured what he - and his buddy - had done for the few miserable coins he had shown. It was enough for Paul to become very smug; He completely overlooked the humbling fact that it was not long since he would have done the same thing for the same end.

As there was nothing to be gained by any further talk with this group, he took the path that led beyond the rock behind which Billy and his cohorts had gone without returning. The picture gathered from the group indicated that the 'place' lay in that direction, with the distance rather vague. There was also a thread of discomfort - fear? Enough to make him wonder at the wisdom of pushing on. He tried to clarify that, but all he could get was someone ranting and raving while everyone cowered from him. So, this little group had reason to fear this unknown person. Before much longer, he was to find out first-hand all about him.

The glade was quickly left behind him as he made his way through the gathering gloom and increasingly stark landscape. He saw no-one, but there were a few shadows here and there. Only twice was he held up. The first was when he heard a sound behind him. He whirled around to see two men bearing down on him. Both had large cudgels, and both meant business even after their discovery. Paul remained calm, and just as they were upon him, he disappeared from before them and transported to a tree behind them.

He listened to lurid curses from the frustrated muggers as they cast about for him. Paul was tempted to play with them but wisely decided not to, for no better reason than what Sean had said,

"The trouble with Mankind is that he is in the state he is in because he always misuses his powers to the detriment of others, and in the end, to himself as well. So, in retaining your natural abilities, you must use them wisely and well, or you will find yourself once more on the slippery slope to finish up where you were before you came here. You will find yourself back to square one, as I believe you say."

The exercise was valuable training, however, and he was beginning to acquire good reflexes, which gave a boost to his confidence. Also, he realised that here was a possible source of information. The robbers had almost given up in disgust, when Paul called to them, showing himself and beckoning them.

"Put your clubs down and come over here! Come on; I want to talk to you! I'm not a ghost, and I'm not going to hurt you! Are you scared of me?" The last question did it. So incensed that they closed the gap between them, and although they lowered the clubs, they kept them at the ready.

"We're not scared of you! You might be one of those queer jokers that disappear all the time, but we're not scared of you. Why do you do that?"

Paul spread his arms and gave a short bark of laughter, "Am I supposed to stand here and let you two hooligans bash me into a pulp? Not bloody likely!"

A look of startled surprise flashed across their faces! "Yeah! Yeah! Never thought of that! But how do you do it? If we leave you alone and don't try to rob you, will you teach us how?"

"I haven't got time to teach you!" Paul was reluctant to have anything to do with them. He knew that without a radical change in the outlook and attitude of these people, nothing would happen, and they were here precisely because their awareness was at this level and would remain so until something or someone touched them on that trigger spot which would bring that metamorphosis from ignorant, brutish men to acknowledged children of God, willing to accept their true origin.

What Paul was becoming aware of was his own changing ideas and attitudes. Before he came to these realms of Spirit, he would have taken every opportunity to exact a heavy penalty on anyone who tried to 'do' him. His aim had been to do unto others before they could do to you, and if any tried to do him, they could expect immediate retaliation. Now, he was more inclined to ask why was he under attack. In this case, robbery, of course, but why? Now he was much more concerned with their plight than his own. With a flash of insight, of awakening beingness, humility, and conscience, he could now see some of the entire mural of existence.

Their actions sprang from ignorance, for they had yet to learn that theft and the use of force was quite unnecessary. If they but knew it, they could have whatever they desired. However, they would probably take some time to understand that while they might satisfy all their lower appetites, they would be on the slippery slope into more and more degradation.

Here were two beings, the product of their individual experience. For whatever reason, be it misdirection by those who pretend to know, or by greed and hedonism largely fostered by the nihilism preached by others. In fact, when he found out who some of these 'others' were, he could not refrain from a little grin. Another piece of the picture would fall into place.

These two were now in this unfortunate state, which brought him to wonder whether these two were asleep, children, or fools, to the definition Sean had given. If they were asleep, or children, he could possibly help, but there was little chance of that if they were fools. By now, he well understood the maxim of not casting seed on stony ground. However, a question or two might be worthwhile. He asked, "Do either of you know where you are or why you're here?" He was met by two blank stares. One of them answered at last. "We dunno where this is. Do you know?"

"That depends on whether you know you're both dead. Do you know that?

"Dead? Dead? How in hell can we be dead! Look! We got arms, legs, heads! And where's the angels? Or the devils and fires and things? There ain't nothin' like that here! How can we be dead?" they both hooted with laughter.

Paul stood with a little smile of understanding and said quietly, "Alright! If you don't know and don't want to know, I'm just wasting my time trying to teach you anything." And he turned away. "Hold on!" One of the pair grabbed Paul by the arm, "What makes you think we're dead?" Paul said quietly, "Take your hand off my arm!" The man did as he was bid before he realised he had done it and stepped back in confusion. "Thank you," Paul maintained in his quiet voice, "Because you are in the realm where people go when they die. You died, and that's why you're here. But I see you can't accept that little truth…"

"You're just trying to fool us! You're trying to trap us or something! I've never heard anything so bloody stupid!"

"So be it!" Paul said over his shoulder and strode off.

The robbers tried to grab him again, but he got the message a fraction before the action and was well away, leaving the fools raving in frustration behind. He was right, of course. There was nothing to be gained by trying to penetrate such a density of nonthought.

He would not be caught unawares again, for he had become much more sensitive to thought patterns around him. He knew now that he was virtually surrounded by potential attackers, but none dared to try, for in some manner he could not explain, he had developed a degree of invulnerability. Beneath the predator's clamour, however, there was an undercurrent of fear, or uncertainty and a longing so intense as to make him stop to try to identify it. He cast about but at first, could see nothing. The feelings became stronger in one area, however, so moving in that direction, he almost fell over them.

They were two girls and a man, all huddled together and crouching so low as to be almost invisible. They looked fearfully up at him, who could not be other than affected by their plight. One girl - she could not be more than fifteen years or so spoke up in a tremulous whisper, "Sir, can you help us? We've been here for a long time waiting..." The other girl interrupted, "Are you an angel?" "Good grief, no!" Paul, surprised at such an idea, gave a little embarrassed giggle, "Oh, no, I'm not an angel. I'm just looking for a friend who's here somewhere." The first girl spoke up again, "They told us there would be angels and golden streets, and harps, and things..." She lapsed into silence for a moment, "But, we've been here since our boat sank, oh, for ages." She began to sob.

"Tell me what happened." Paul crouched beside them, "I might be able to help, if you can tell me about yourselves." The young girl wailed and clung to the other girl. "We're dead, aren't we? We were drowned, I think." "Tell me what happened," he insisted firmly but kindly.

"We were in this lifeboat, see, because our ship was on fire. Then this storm came up, and we got thrown into the sea because it was bad." She paused to blow her nose. "Then I think we were drowned because none of us can swim. Then we woke up here. We did drown, didn't we? And isn't this supposed to be heaven? Or is it...the other place?"

"No, not quite, although there are much nicer places than this. But how long do you think you've been here? It can't have been long, surely. You would have been noticed by now." The older girl replied, "It seems like hours, but it's hard to tell. There's nothing here to judge time by." She was a little more composed than her companion, and gave more details, "We woke up with our friend here, but he's still out. Is he dead?"

Paul answered with a little grin, "We're all dead here! Some, just a bit more dead than others!" They were a trifle shocked at that. "It's no joke!" the young one cried, "I didn't want to die! I've got a lifetime of living to do yet! Now look at me," she wailed in her misery. "I didn't mean to upset you," he was contrite, "But really, you can enjoy yourself here when you learn something about yourself... That is, if you want to know." "Tell us! Tell us!" they both clamoured.

"Steady on! I can't tell you everything in two minutes!" He held up his hands in mock horror, "But I can give you a bit to go on with. Then we'll see."

"You're dead. You understand that?" They both nodded. "We must be, or we would've been rescued and taken to a strange place," the older girl said.

"So, you're dead, because so am I, and everyone else you meet here as well," he went on to tell them about their spiritual life, that death was only a transition from one state of existence to another. He told them about their new bodies, their new surroundings, and something of their potential. He finished by saying, "If you want more, I'll contact a friend, and he will know what to do." The older of the two girls listened carefully; the more he said, the more distraught she became. Finally, she burst into tears.

"Oh God, have mercy on my soul! Oh Mary, Mother of God, save me! Oh, Mary, Mother of God, save me from perdition?" Paul tried to calm her, but she was too upset. It transpired that she had died without absolution, and she was terrified of her fate. Paul knew there was only one thing he could do. He excused himself for a few moments as he composed his mind, concentrating on contacting Sean, who would know what to do.

"What's up, Lad?" And here he was! Paul quickly explained, a little embarrassed for asking. Sean smiled, "You did right; I can help her seeing that I am a priest. Introduce me as such, and we'll pull her out of this."

Paul hastened to comply, and the look of gratitude on the girl's face was reward enough. Sean knelt beside the girl, took her hand, and Paul left them to it. As expected, Sean very soon had her tears changing to tears of joy.

"Good work, Paul!" He gripped his arm, "Now, I'll take care of these lost ones while you carry on with your little quest. Any problems?"

"No, nothing I can't handle." Then he realised just what he had said. He just asked for help, and now he was saying the opposite. Sean put him at ease.

"You did handle it! You did the right thing. I'll see you later!" And he gathered up the little group, huddled them up tight, and they all vanished, leaving Paul to himself.

Without further incident, he came across what seemed a very common feature in these parts; a wall surrounding a group of crude buildings. Even the wall was crude. A good push would knock it over. He walked along looking for a way in, aware that he was being watched, but he ignored it.

Then he came to a place where the wall had collapsed, and he could see into the compound. Ugly and stinking, it reflected the level of the inhabitants. The people he saw were in deep apathy, showing no interest in him at all. He stood a while pondering on the difference between the would-be robbers who had accosted him and these poor wretches.

Was this level of personal degradation in keeping with their previous lifestyles? Had they been the ones who lived on the fruits of the toil of honest folk? Were they greedy, selfish, uncaring of any but themselves? Likely some, or all of that, he thought, and he grimaced as he realised how close he had been to joining these moribund creatures, if there were such among the dead! Here they were, no status, no energy, no hope, for this was their own evaluation of themselves. A voice broke his reverie.

"Hey! What yer starin' at? What's your business? You come to see the boss?" It was a tall gangling man, gaunt and ragged, with a club held menacingly. The man kept his distance; for all his bluster he was afraid of Paul. Then he took a course strange to him. Previously he would have given as good, or better, than he got, meeting belligerence with a similar manner. Now he found himself relaxed, smiling and even polite.

"No, I don't want to see the boss." He replied in a casual tone, "I've come looking for an old friend who might be here. His name..." He stopped as he saw a line of heavies forming behind the lanky one, who raised his club as Paul had taken a step forward. The others followed suit. Paul's confidence faded a little; it was all he could do to maintain his poise. There was something tragic even bordering on the ridiculous about the scene.

Paul could only stand and stare as the man screamed, "Come any closer and we'll bash you head in! You're one of those Bible-Basher's, I'll bet! We don't want your sort around here!

"Why are you afraid of me? I'm unarmed as you can see" He spread his hands. "How can I possibly hurt you!?" "Oh! The man laughed a funny little broken laugh, I've seen your sort in action before. You're not to be trusted, that's what the boss sez. You're no good 'ere!"

"Can I come in and see if my friend is here? That's all I want, and as I said, I don't have any weapons," He stood there, calm and relaxed without fear or anxiety. He felt completely at ease, in control of the situation despite their damn great clubs. He had nothing other than the confidence of his ability. He also sensed that under their bluster and threats there was something close to superstitious fear. They were mortally afraid of him.

Of immediate concern was to win enough confidence to gain entrance without raising any more opposition. One way would be to cross their palms with silver - no, gold would be better. No good, he thought regretfully, no gold! He wished he had the coins Jane had been given. Nice, heavy gold coins! He could picture them in his hand, three lovely coins about three centimetres in diameter with something that could be a head on one side and on the tails side something like a coat-of-arms. Then he almost dropped them in surprise, for here they were! They were real and heavy in his hand. Three gold coins, the same as Jane had in his hand, the clinking of which very quickly drew the attention of the club brigade.

"I can pay my way," Paul jingled the coins, "does that change your mind?"

"Let's take a look at what you got," demanded the thin man. "If you've got the real stuff, well, maybe!" he shrugged, "Maybe you can come in. Give us a look first"

Paul tossed him a coin which he caught expertly, hefted it in his hand, bit it and peered at it carefully before saying, "Where did you get gold like this? He was suspicious, "Ain't never seen any like this. Did you rob someone?" Paul saw he could gain more by playing along with these characters; he would not get very far without their help.

"Something like that," he said dismissively, "The thing is, can you help me?" A greedy leer crossed the man's face. "You got any more? How much's your friend worth?" "Just let me in, and I'll do the rest" He went to take a confident pace forward, but stopped in mid-stride as a bellow made the small crowd cower away from where the voice came.

"What the hell's goin' on here? Who the hell are you? What do you want?" A huge powerful-looking man appeared. He was dressed in little more than rags, in keeping with the others. He carried a whip which by his attitude got a fair amount of use. He worked the coils in his hands as he glared about, finally resting on Paul.

"Well? You! I'm talking to you! Who the hell are you, and what do you want?" He scowled fiercely.

Paul was taken aback by this big brute. He must have been someone to keep clear of back on the Earth-plane. That whip had been considerably used and was probably long enough to reach him. Poised for instant flight, he managed to appear relaxed as he replied,

"I have come to look for a friend of mine who I think could be here. Do you mind if I come into your town?"

"Let's get a good look at you." the big man growled,

"Are you one of those bastards who come here and tells us weird things about being dead, and other lies like that?"

Paul was not too keen on stepping forward; he knew he could not trust him, and that most certainly applied to the others as well; taking a small step, he replied, "Do I look like one? What do they look like, anyway?" He saw he had gone too far as the man's knuckles whitened as he gripped the whip, "So! A cocky young pup in fancy-dress! A proper bloody-little pansy! A poof! Let's see if you can dance!"

In a lightning-fast motion, he uncoiled the whip in a snake-like, lunge at Paul's feet. But he had seen both his thought and his body language. The whip cracked on empty air. Paul was out of reach, standing, considering his next move. His mind was made up for him.

The giant, seeing Paul evade the whip, charged, yelling, "Why, you dogs' vomit! I'll teach you!" So, he vanished, leaving the man raving in frustration, ordering his men, under dire threats, to find him. But Paul was up a tree, literally. He didn't expect them to look up, and he was right. Up in the tree, he now had time to plan his next move. He thought he should be invisible but didn't like skulking about, and he was not at all sure of how he might maintain such a state.

"Find him!" the big man screamed, "Find that louse! No man puts one over on Jack the giant!" The remainder of his tirade was laced with a stream of obscenities the like of which Paul had never heard. Several impossible things were to be done to parts of his anatomy when he was caught, something he was determined to avoid. He could not help thinking how he could never have escaped from such as these when he first ran away from Thomas, John, Jessie and company. He found himself being very grateful to Sean for all his valuable teaching.

With a little concentration, he was able to picture himself as a cardboard cut-out, and aligning himself with the line of vision of the searchers, he would remain undetected. He was very pleased; he was actually able to follow instructions, and successfully as well. He recalled almost verbatim the words Sean used:

"Note, young Paul, in gaining the growth available to those who seek it, you learn that Thought is everything. Without it there can be nothing. Absolutely nothing."

"The existence of realms, spiritual planes, physical worlds, everything, the totality of existence, is the result of Thought. Your state of being, your location, whatever you see, touch, taste, all is the result of considerations made and agreed upon, or perhaps, just agreed on."

"This, if you can but grasp it, is the one thing which will open all doors, with the qualification that one must have cleaned up his karma, so to speak. That cannot really be done here; one must return to the physical realm to do that. Since the deeds which earned that debt were incurred on that plane, back you must go to work off that debt.

Remember, too, that all physical-plane lives, all incarnations, are learning periods as well, and while the process seems circular, there is one important difference and that is each time 'round raises your level, just as the thread of a screw works."

That was how, he realised, the coins appeared. He did it. His movement out of reach of the whip was similar. He did it. All these things happened because he did it. He further reasoned that he could not do these things on Earth, even when he first arrived in these realms, because everyone knew you can't do these things. If you try, you fail because you expect to fail. There is a large mass of muddle thinking from countless incidents reaching back thousands of incarnations on Earth, and other places as well.

For some this mass is well-nigh impenetrable either from without, or within, preventing any creative thoughts from being effective, as a wall shuts off light. Earth style thoughts are therefore so solid, so encysted as to be impervious. One must be a true Master on Earth to do what Paul was doing here, and he knew he was no master. So, how has he overcome the barriers? When Sean told him on his return why this was, so he marvelled at the simplicity of it.

Right now, there was more afoot than sitting up a tree pondering on the nature of thoughts and thinking. He was abruptly brought back to the present by a shout. One of the club-bearers was below Paul, pointing upwards and yelling. What he had overlooked was that only from two directions was a cardboard man invisible. This searcher had move to one side, and of course he could be seen now.

So, what to do? He had no desire to be captured even when he could escape easily. There was little use in maintaining the mental picture. "Hey! Another realisation hit him. A mental picture! Ha! All these profound things turn out to be so simple!"

But there was little time for that. The tree was already trembling with climbers. Jack the Giant, was screaming at his men, while others watched from the safety of the huts. That's the place to be Paul thought, so he went there in a blink. He was getting used to such rapid movement and could not squash a little smirk of satisfaction.

There were quite a few peering around the huts. But this time, he remained unseen, remembering what had happened last time. Standing among the people he listened to the comments, mostly bitter, noncomplimentary, and not a few, very rude.

They were all afraid of this Jack the Giant, and they were terrified of his whip. Paul had to know why they stayed. What was keeping them in this hellhole?

Moving to a point behind the main throng he relaxed his guard and stood, clearly seen, but out of sight of the searchers, now up the trees and growing more frantic under the curses of the giant.

"Hm! Hm!" He cleared his throat, at which one, then another spun round, gasping in surprise and shock. Any stranger was cause for grave suspicion. He looked over this woe-begone pathetic lot, all in rags, filthy and gaunt. One man demanded querulously, "Who the hell are you?" the man next to him snarled, "He's the one! He's the one they're after! And he's got gold! I seen it!" He made a lunge at Paul, and this time he was too slow. He was grabbed on each side by these stinking thieves.

"Come on! Hand it over! We know you got it!"

"Take your hands off me!" Paul commanded in a firm voice. As he spoke, he shook himself. The two holding him yelled in surprise and dropped his arms in pain, rubbing their hands, glaring in puzzlement and not a little fear. Paul had given them a shock, generated exactly as any other mental picture. It was most effective. One of the men raised his fist menacingly and growled between his teeth, "You little squirt! I'll..." Paul held up his hand and said softly but firmly, "Back off! I've come here for one thing only – to look for a friend. I have no weapons, and I mean no harm to anyone, even your big bully." As he spoke, he reached into his pocket, "Here! Take the gold! It's no use to me. Have you anywhere to spend it?" The man caught the two coins by reflex action as Paul tossed them to him, looked in puzzled surprise, then a huge grin showed his delight. An immediate scuffle broke out as the others tried to take them off him. Paul ignored them; there was little time left, for the searchers were on their way back. He asked the ones not involved in the skirmish,

"Do any of you know a man called Arthur White? Usually, called Snow? Tallish, fair, and probably about twenty or so." Those who heard him, looked at one another, and shuffled their feet.

One girl shrugged and muttered, "Yeah, I know him, I think. Always in trouble, he is. Big Jack whipped him and threw him in the cooler."

"What for?" Paul asked.

"Getting too sassy! He's always answering back, and Jack don't stand for none of that! Ooo! He got a real goin' over, and no mistake!"

"Where is it? The cooler?"

"That one there!" She pointed to a shack a few metres down the 'street,' "But, you better be careful! Jack's not one to fool about with. Anyhow," she pressed herself against him and looked with appealing eyes, "What's in it for me? Worth a little reward, isn't it?"

Beneath the unkempt appearance he could see what would have been a very attractive girl. Another hooker? He didn't know, but her manner suggested she was. However, he had other things on his mind. He could give her a coin, perhaps, but not here, not surrounded by desperate people all broadcasting a mixture of fear, distrust, greed, and utter hopelessness.

These wretches here were very much worse off than the lot at Elija's corral; these were indeed getting down to the bottom of the barrel. The pity of it all was their own ignorance, and this, as the basis for their lack of trust, leading to a lack of regard for each other brought a state of existence more savage and brutal than anyone would find on the Earth-plane.

He also knew now what kept this lot in this place. Not Jack the Giant! No, simply, there was nowhere else to go! If they left, some other power-hungry yobo would very quickly snatch them up as his own personal slaves.

But even here, in the darkest of the areas yet seen by him, he felt there were some who would listen to him, if he attempted a rescue. He could not help noticing one girl standing out from the others. She looked gentle and somehow aloof from the rest. She took a little step towards Paul, wanting to say something.

But, right now, things were rapidly hotting up as Jack and his lot came around the corner, and the group around Paul melted away, leaving him standing clear. Big Jack snarled as he approached, "Got you now, pretty boy!"

His whip snaked out, whistling through the air. Paul stood his ground, grateful for the realisation that Sean was whispering in his ear, "Freeze them! then you can talk!" Unseen but very welcome, he pressed Paul on the shoulder. In mid-stroke, with an upraised arm, Big Jack stopped, frozen in his tracks. He could growl, but not move. None of them could, and all but Jack were stunned into silence.

He screamed, "What have you done to me? Let me go! I'll kill you! Let me go!" Paul stood, calmly waiting for him to wind down, but Jack gave no sign of stopping. To assist in pacifying him, Paul went over to him and relieved him of his whip.

"Do you think I'm about to stand here and let you thrash me?" Carefully keeping his voice as neutral as possible, he looked over the frozen tableau, where one man caught in mid-stride and unable to save himself had fallen.

"I have not come here to threaten anyone, and I will not be threatened by anyone! I have come in peace, and in peace, I shall leave. I am here to look for a friend. I am told he may be in your cooler. If so, I would like you to release him, for I understand he has done nothing more than tell the truth. He called you a big bully, did he not."

Jack grew red with rage, embarrassment, and not a little fear as he spluttered, "You...you...Wait till I get you! I'll..." What he would do was cut off by his scream of sheer terror as he slowly rose a metre or so off the ground.

"Do I hear your order to release my friend?" This went unheard by Big Jack as he howled to be let down. Paul finally had to freeze his voice as well as his muscles long enough to get his request across. Jack tried desperately to nod in eager agreement, terrified by his suspension.

"You can speak now if you don't shout and curse. What do you want to say?"

"Let me down! Let me down!" he shrieked. He tried to wriggle free, but he was quite immobile.

"When you give the order to release my friend, you can come down. Not before!"

"Alright! Alright! Let him go, for chrissake! Let him go! And let me down!" Paul had inadvertently hit on one of Big Jack's phobias. He was terrified of heights. Or was it accidental?

A chuckle from Sean, still quite close to Paul's shoulder, made him wonder. And there were, as usual, more questions that needed answering. Sean's thoughts seemed to grin, if that were possible, and he said, "All in good time!" and was no longer present. Had he done all these things, frozen these yobos, and raised Jack?

Over at the gaol, a door opened, and a tall figure staggered out.

"Snow! Over here! Snow!" The figure turned and slowly walked stiffly over to Paul, with Jack, and his minders standing open-mouthed. As Snow approached, Jack's feet touched the ground, and he immediately charged. Or rather, he attempted to charge. He looked as if he was stuck in glue, for he could not move his feet more than a few inches.

Snow slowed his already slow approach as he looked around suspiciously. He saw Jack, unexpectedly subdued, as were his minders, tamed by this little figure firmly in command. He stopped two or three paces away, looking at Paul, who had a huge grin on his face.

"Hi! Remember me?" Snow peered at the speaker, and slowly a look of puzzled pleasure lit his face.

"Paul? Is it you? Paul Askew? How the hell did you end up here? Paul laughed, and extended his arms, unashamedly embracing his old mate. He looked much the same, though rather gaunt. In answer to his question, he replied, "Easy! Easy as falling off a hill!" He quickly explained what had happened, but there was little time for talk. Big Jack was roaring again, "Alright! Alright! I've let him go! What about me?"

Paul could see just what he had in mind. He made a face, "If I let you go now, you're going to try to grab us. Are you not? I see it in your mind's eye. I'm right, aren't I?"

He could see only too clearly that was so. He swept them all with a calm gaze, "Have you lot ever seen someone who honours his word? When someone makes a statement, do you not believe him? I told you I come in peace, with malice or harmful intent to none, not even your Jack the Giant here. I don't threaten him or you. I have provoked no attack, unless disobedience to Jack here is provoking him. If so, he has a lot to learn. He has no authority whatsoever over any of you, unless you let him."

"Challenge his power, and it will disappear like melting snow. Allow him to bully you, and he will do just that."

"Now, my task here is complete; I have my friend, and we will be leaving in a few moments. If there are any here who wish for a better life than here, I will take you with us. I can promise something better than this if you want it. But no questions now - you will have to trust me."

"Anyone who wants to come, follow us!" He took Snow by the elbow and started off, past the still inert club-bearers who could do nothing but glower. As they passed, Paul spoke over his shoulder, "Only those who want to, can come with us. The rest of you cannot move until we are out of sight."

He was very surprised to see two of the club-bearers join them as they moved off; he had to wonder if they were merely looking for a quick advantage, a perk or two. He knew it would show later; their manner and behaviour would sort them out.

There was quite a group. At least half of the population, it seemed, went along. A motley bunch they were, too. All seemed about the same age, late twenties-early thirties, men and women, some hurling abuse at the minders, at Jack himself, and at the entire miserable set-up. Paul was pleased to see the girl who had attracted his attention also in the group. One or two were eager to exact vengeance for the treatment received, but Paul managed to dissuade them by telling them not to descend to their level.

Paul had been right in reading Jack's intentions. The moment they were out of sight around some trees, there was the sound of pursuit. But by the time the roughs rounded the bend, the entire group was nowhere to be seen.

With the swift aid of Sean, always nearby, they were whisked away and placed, as one person, in the square of the village from which Paul had set out. "How did you do that?" Snow let out a huge whoosh of breath, "Can you work miracles? Where is this place?"

As he spoke, the girl Paul had noticed came and stood beside him. Snow gave her a little hug as he said, "This is my sister Jennifer." Paul looked in astonishment, "You haven't got a sister!"

"Oh yes I have!" Snow laughed, "And here she is. "But it's a long story. I'll tell you later. But where is this place?"

A familiar voice made Paul spin around, to see Jane coming at the run. "Paul! Oh, Paul! You've come back!" she cried, "Oh, I'm glad you're alright!" He laughed, "Why wouldn't I be?" as he embraced her, "What could happen to me? I've had Sean hovering over my shoulder most of the time - thank goodness!" "And you've brought your friend!" She turned to Snow, "And I'm glad you did!" she said over her shoulder to Paul and looked back to Snow, "But I seem to know you already, but I don't know why."

In the flurry of bringing a bunch of new folk in, there was little time for further talk, and there was much to be done to settle them in. So, for the next indefinite period, Paul was totally involved in lecturing, teaching, and explaining to any who would listen, any who wanted to learn something.

As the teaching progressed, Snow became angrier. "Do you mean to say that there are people back home, back on Earth, who know all about these things? And that others work all their lives to stop us poor bastards from knowing the truth? I must accept what you say, because I know now these things have happened, just as you said. But I'd almost like to get back there and sort a few people out! I know of one or two who need a wake-up! When you die, you go to Heaven, do you? Ha! Well, this is a hell of a lot better than where we were. And you say there's a place a lot better than this? How do we get there?"

Paul gave a little shrug, and a little rueful grin, "I'm not quite sure yet. Sean tells us it's only a matter of development and growth, and I'm not quite sure what that means. You know Moira, of course, well she's there now, and I've seen her once or twice, and she's told me a little bit about what it's like. We've both got a bit of work to do, I think, but Sean said not to try to rush it; there's the whole of time ahead of us, but there is no real worry about anything. You know Sean told you this was the area many come to after body death because while they are not developed to be able to accept the higher planes, they were not villains, not bad people, not criminals, just unaware of the truth about themselves."

"The bad ones, the real villains, those without honour or respect for anyone else were confined - by their own outlook to where Big Jack is. They know of no other places, and they cannot ever come here, let alone any higher planes."

During this period, Paul was surprised, looking back to the time of his arrival on the Plane of Spirit, just how much he had learnt with the subsequent changes in his outlook. He now knew a little about himself, and mankind in general, this place in the Cosmos, and something of his responsibilities. He pondered a little on the timing of his Earthly demise, for he had died young. There must've been some reason. If not, there was something missing in his understanding of things. It was not just a series of random events; all these things 'just happened' without any reason. One thing he recalled, however, helped to bind all these things together, more than some thought he knew existed. He recalled the words of a writer, who said,

"Here is a test to see if your task on Earth is completed. If you're alive, it isn't."

So, he was dead. To the Earth-plane, that was. So, his work, whatever that was, had been finished. If that were so, what had been his purpose? He was learning a great deal here, and that was fine, but in leaving that 'life,' particularly so early, was his task completed?

Sean, as usual, was the source of some good advice. "There are two main answers to this, my hungry-minded boy: a yes and a no. Yes, because we all make plans well in advance of any events, often many years ahead. We choose our parents, which will decide our circumstances for that incarnation, to pay a particular debt or to learn a lesson, as it could be both. We plan our Time of birth, often our marital partner, the time of our death, and our return here where the planning took place, oh, many years before."

He continued, "So, when we allow a wild factor to enter the computation, it's a source of wonder, pride, and even humility, when we realise that of all the creations of our Father-Mother God, we are the only ones who have been granted the power of choice. Therefore, if we decide - for whatever reason - to act a certain way which turns out contrary to our main plan, you might have decided to be a baker, say, when you wind up being a butcher, making it much more difficult, even impossible, to reach that goal. If so, we will one day find we must repeat that series of actions until we, at last, make it and reach that goal."

"The thing is, we must do this as many times as necessary."

"So," Paul rubbed his chin, "We make these plans before birth, then we find, for any reason whatever, we take another direction. Is that right?"

"That can be right," Sean grinned, "But also don't forget, that sometimes we follow our charted course. To the letter. The same goes for tests of many kinds that we are confronted with. Tests we must pass to allow further development. If we fail, and of course we do, many times, that test is presented to us again and again until we struggle through."

"That, dear boy, is why we are going through this seemingly endless cycle of life after life, and of course, not forgetting Karmic reasons. All debts must be paid in full, and none may escape. Really, it comes down to physical life, Earth-style, for learning and settling accounts, and these realms for all the out-of-school activities, for some pleasant recreation, and battery charging, I think you call it."

"And every turn, every cycle, raises the person further up the ladder, as the thread on a screw spirals upwards. Now, off you go and play for a while, but don't forget your homework!"

Cross Communication

Alice White awoke that morning feeling strange. Something had happened during the night. She had had this peculiar dream. She had been with friends the previous evening and had a shade more to drink than was prudent, a little more than a shade, really. She had staggered into bed a little before midnight and had dropped into a deep sleep instantly, as one would expect with a fair cargo of gin on board.

Sometime after that, she started to dream. She dreamt that her son, killed many months before, had stood by her bed, with several others, telling her something. She crept into the kitchen, trying not to jolt her aching head, feeling rotten and vowing never to touch the stuff again, clumsily making herself a cup of coffee.

She sat, feeling slightly better with the coffee and a fag, trying to remember what that damn dream was about, but it eluded her. She was a product of her society; solidly materialistic, not particularly religious, and quite happy to go along with the general trend. Things like don't have any way-out ideas, look after number one, make sure you're alright, and above all, don't think! It's too painful!

Therefore, the idea of going to a spiritualist church was something she would never dream of doing. All her friends would laugh, for starters! But this disconnected phrase kept coming up – 'spiritualist church' - and whenever she wasn't thinking of anything, this bloody thing kept cropping up. In exasperation, she took a shower, got dressed, and decided to visit her best friend.

The short walk to her friend's place helped her considerably. It was a nice spring morning, with that undefinable something in the air. By the time she arrived at her friend's, she had just about decided that all this was a load of rubbish, and she forgot about it. With good company, more coffee, and a good chat, she was even able to forget her hangover.

Feeling a good deal better about life in general, she settled back, with everything as it should be, allowing for incompetent politicians, taxes, robberies, increasing violence, rapes, and what could you do about it anyway?

Sean nodded in satisfaction. They - Snow, Paul, and Sean watched as Alice White moved in her sleep as if a mite restless, then sighed, turned over and dropped back into deeper sleep.

It had started when Snow came to Paul. "Can we go somewhere? There're one or two things..." Paul nodded and took him to a small rise overlooking the village.

"What's up?" Paul asked of his friend.

"I guess you might think I'm going a bit soft," he sounded embarrassed, looking everywhere but at Paul, "Do you know how I can get in touch with my mother? One of the guys I met was going on about how he was talking to his wife through someone he called a... a clear-something. Do you know anything about it and how it's done?"

"Don't be shy about it!" Paul laughed, "It's perfectly natural to want to contact your mother. I wish I could get to mine, but she would never go to a medium or clairvoyant – that's the word you wanted - and that's the best way to do it. You can contact them sometimes while they sleep, but they think they only dreamt it and can't accept it as proof you're actually still alive. Oh yes, it's quite possible."

"All we have to do is give her the idea of going to one of the spiritualist churches, and if she does that, we can do the rest," Paul explained.

"Why can't I contact her direct? I can go there, can't I? I mean, we're all spirits, so your friend Sean says. So, we should be able to talk the way we do here."

"Yes, right! But you remember what people say about things like that; all they do is scoff and laugh their heads off at such codswallop. When you're in that sort of society, it takes a person braver than the rest to talk about such things. Remember, back there; you're only a meat body, nothing else. They have never seen what you can see right now - a spirit body, so there's nothing to survive when the body croaks, so most people go along with the mob, never asking, never daring to. Even the parson gives you a funny look if you ask him. So only a few are really willing to look."

Paul continued, "When they do, many of them get a big surprise. There's enough indisputable evidence about now; I'm told many have known for over a hundred years or so, that they are something more than a mere body, and that something survives their body's demise."

"And the spiritualist movement holds regular meetings all over the world, and they have sensitive people who can actually talk to beings such as us, and more to the point, we can talk to them," Paul concluded.

Snow had been listening avidly to all that and, at first, was very keen, but after a moment, he slumped despondently. "Yeah, but how do we get her to go? She'll never go to one of those places!"

"No harm in trying, is there? Sean says there's not much to it, really."

"How in hell do you know so much, anyway? I've been here a lot longer than you, and I know nothing!" Snow retorted.

"Oh, I'm lucky! I've got a very good teacher! He's been giving me all this info as I tell you about it, and he also says that there are times when it's necessary to try to influence someone still incarnate, you know, alive on Earth, to do something. But he also says that it must be done with a great deal of care. It must never ever be for anything but helpful reasons; there are only too many who would scream 'satanic forces at work.' Another important reason for great care is that if we - from this end - do it in any way that might result in hurt for someone, Sean says we add to our own karmic debt, something to be settled - paid back – that is."

Sean sauntered over to where they were talking, "Paul, why don't you and Arthur take a little trip to the Earth-plane to see if you can see one of these mediums in action? Then you might see just how this works."

"Hadn't thought of that," Paul replied, "Where do you suggest we go?"

"Oh, several likely places. London is always a good one. But since you're both from New Zealand, why not try there? I've heard there are one or two very good mediums there," Sean responded.

"Yes," Paul was a bit doubtful, "But how do we get there?" Sean smiled, "The same way you came back from that ghastly place; just go! That's all!"

So, they went. And it was just like that. Just as simple. Oh, they had to scout around a little, but they found a place to which, much to their surprise, they were attracted by the powerful feeling of friendship, togetherness; there seemed an aura of enlightenment, of certainty, of serenity and peace.

There were about thirty people present, seated in a room, apparently waiting for someone or something. They were relaxed and friendly, chatting away. There was to be a service, but there was none of the usual dour silence one would find in most established churches. There was even quite a bit of banter flying about. Then two people emerged from a room and took their places at a table placed before the main group.

As Paul and Arthur stood, or rather, floated around the room, they could see them quite well, albeit rather dimly. Good enough for Arthur to recognise a girl. "Hey! Do you remember her?" Arthur asked Paul, excitedly, "That's Sue Wills, isn't it? Fancy seeing her here!"

Paul tried to shush him, until he realised there was no way she or anyone else could see or hear them. Or was there? The lady who sat at the table looked in their direction, and she must have seen them, for she acknowledged them with a little thought. Shortly after that, she stood up and said she was going to demonstrate clairvoyance. She looked around the room, and suddenly both Paul and Arthur were almost bowled over by several new arrivals from their plane, who all wanted to speak, through her, to someone in the room. But since she had seen Arthur before the others showed up, she went to the girl indicated by Arthur, who was standing behind her, pointing down. He said to the medium,

"Please tell her I hope she passed her exams, and that she should marry Gerald. She'll understand."

To their surprise, the medium passed that on to the girl, who recognised Arthur, accepted his message, and was obviously very pleased one of her past acquaintances would speak to her 'from the grave,' but the medium corrected that idea, with many more contacts made by the visiting throng from the astral plane.

As they watched, they were constantly amazed at the accuracy of the medium, in passing on the information to her recipients, who were, in turn, delighted.

"Well," Snow White grinned, "I never knew any of this was true before. Now, well, I've sure got a lot to learn!"

Back at the village, they both needed a little time in which to digest what they had just seen. There was absolutely no doubt that this medium was totally genuine, and completely at ease with all the disembodied ones. Paul wondered if it might be possible to have a chat with her. Sean answered, "Not normally," He cleared his throat, "If she allowed any of us to talk to her any old time, she would be very busy and also very unhappy. She would have no privacy, no peace, with all of us clamouring to be heard."

"What we have to do is wait until she sits in meditation, and just possibly, we may reach her then. Otherwise, we go unheard because she must switch off, so to speak, during all other times, she is not meditating or doing what she just did. And even then, you will have to convince her guides to allow you near her."

"For her, that is most necessary. Otherwise, she would be inundated."

"Yeah, I see that, but what's with this guide business? I've never had one of those! And..." Snow wondered. "Woah! Steady!" Sean laughed, "Hang on! There's lots I can tell you; give me time!"

"It depends on your personal state of awareness, or development, to know about them. They are with you from birth and hope to do just what they are there for – to guide – when you need it. You may even have several, and one may be more prominent than the others, as each is a specialist in one thing or another. What they cannot do is tell you to do something or make you do it."

"One usually finds they don't come close unless, or until there is an awakening of self-awareness; when you know you're a spirit being, running that body, and that most likely leads to higher awareness."

"Then, your guide may move closer, to be available. Don't forget," He wagged a finger at Snow, "The guide cannot make you do anything! His influence is only for your well-being and advancement. You always make the decision to act, or not to act."

"And of course, in the case of our lady friend, you witnessed her guides… But Snow interrupted, "I saw no guides! There were several people there, close to her, that's all!"

"Ah! Correct! But you don't know who they were, do you? The real problem you had was simply one of observation; they were there all the time, but you were too busy looking at the bods in the room to notice the others."

"Hang on a moment!" Paul objected, "If that's so, who is, or rather, was, my guide?" Sean gave a huge beaming smile and gave a little bow, "At your service, milord!"

Paul stared in total disbelief. He looked, looked away, and looked again. "You?" he whispered; "Then how the hell didn't I know about it"

"Ah! You've forgotten just how materialistic your world was.

Such things as you know about now, were only myths, legends, or, more rudely, a load of crap. Right?" They had to nod. "And as I said," Sean continued, "I couldn't get close for the reasons I said before; you knew nothing about yourself, because, again, this was the world you grew up in."

"What about me then!" demanded Snow, "Did I have one? Jennifer came up just then and, hearing his question, linked into his arm, squeezed it, and said, "Here I am! But as you now know, I couldn't get close to you or really help you."

Snow could do nothing but look at her, his mouth open. "Alright then, you lot!" Sean swept them with his gaze, "How about this little task we want to do; get your mother," He nodded at Snow, "to a meeting, where we can give her proof of your survival. Now, this is what you do..." He outlined the simplicity of it. They were to go to her while she slept; just a little before dawn was always the best time.

And so, they found themselves standing by her bed just at the first lightening of the eastern sky. They were intrigued by Alice White actually floating above her bed, while her body lay inertly in the bed. Her ethereal body turned restlessly, and she seemed to be dreaming. Sean attempted to link with her, and in a moment, they were able to see her dream. She was lying on the bank of a lovely stream, with beautiful flowers and birds about. Paul whispered in a puzzled voice, "She seems to be here, in this realm! Is that right?"

"Indeed, it is," Sean smiled, "Indeed it is! This is now easy! We just appear and give her the message, repeat it several times so she hopefully won't forget, and that's it."

The figure of Alice White opened her eyes to see these strange people leaning over her, one of whom seemed to be her son. The strange thing was that she was dreaming, but she knew it. And they were telling her something she could not hear clearly. Her son seemed to be saying, "Please, Mum! Please go." The link was getting very thin after only a very short time. Then they saw her astral body slip back into the physical. Alice White stirred, opened her eyes, and muttered, "Bloody dream!" But she lay a while trying to recapture the brief glimpse, she got of someone who looked exactly like her son.

It worked. The following Sunday, Alice White was walking along a street she seldom visited. She was going to a friend, and they intended to have dinner together. The evening was fine and mild, and she was glad to be walking. Then she came across a building with a sign across the door "Spiritualist Centre. Meetings every Sunday, Seven PM. All welcome." She could never explain why she turned and entered.

She was met by a friendly man who looked quite normal, although she had no idea what she expected to see.

The large room was full of relaxed, friendly people talking, laughing even. She sat down and was given a little book with songs in it. She couldn't understand the hubbub of voices, people moving about, even embracing each other. Most unusual, she thought. Any time you were in church, you had to be quiet, you didn't smile or talk to someone at the end of the row.

The minister - no, chairman, he said he was, introduced the clairvoyant-medium for the evening; they had a prayer, someone got up and gave a reading from something or other - not the Bible; - they sang a few hymns, all very relaxed and pleasant.

Then it was the medium's turn. Her name was Violet, and she looked completely normal in every way. Instead of looking strange and weird, she wouldn't have got a second glance out in the street. She was as relaxed and friendly as they all were. She called to several men and women with various messages purporting to have come from someone who had died and known the person. The recipients all seemed to accept what was given, and one man was so moved by what he was told that tears were streaming down his cheeks. He was told his late wife was there in the room; she was well and happy. It was too much for the man. Furthermore, she was identified to him in an unmistakable way.

Alice White sat fascinated by it all. It seemed so natural and easy. Was it all true? She was abruptly shaken out of her thoughts by the medium who called to her, "The lady with the red scarf at the end of the row - can I hear your voice?"

"Who, me?" she stuttered. "Yes, you, my dear. I have two men here with me; one tells me he is your son - he passed to the higher realm about two years ago, and the other is his friend who went off the road in his car. He and his girlfriend went together."

"Your son wants to tell you, he is well and sends his love, and for you to take better care of yourself. He asks if you remember when he skinned his knee falling from a tree onto a fence and to remember what you said at the time. You said he'd break his neck, that he was always hurting himself. And the time you gave him a red jersey." Alice White again nodded, this time in astonishment. All that was exactly right. The medium had one more little snippet to add. "He also says if you look in his book, 'A Coral Island,' you will find a note he wrote once when he was going to run away. If you still have the book, of course."

"I hope you find his coming, a comfort. That's all!" The

remainder of the service was a blur. She had been told things that only she and her son could possibly know. She had found the note in the book when she was going through his things after his death. All of this added up to...she hardly dared think of what it all really meant.

As the service was ending, the chairman invited any who had received messages to stay if they wished and talk to Violet. Alice decided she would and, at the first opportunity, asked her, "Can you describe the one who came to me?" The Medium thought a moment. "He would be tall, maybe six feet, a scar on his chin. He said his name was Arthur, but everyone called him Snow... I suppose..."

"Yes, we often had a good giggle over that," Alice was having some trouble keeping her voice even: this was quite a shock, discovering that her only son was not much further away than an impossibly thin veil of consciousness. "Snow! That's right! Did the man with him give his name as well?"

"Yes, he said his name was Paul, and they had been to school together." She had to accept what the medium said; there was a little option, as what she said about Snow was perfectly correct. But how? How could someone she had never seen before, come up with all of this? She remembered Paul; she had known him quite well in the days the boys knocked about together. But how did the medium know?

"The two men were here, and they spoke to me. Quite simple, really."

"You mean they were ghosts?" Alice asked doubtfully. "In a way," the medium laughed, "You could say that, but they weren't quite what most people think of as ghosts. That is a convenient name to hang on to, something only vaguely understood. Do you see that sign up there?" She pointed to a large banner that proclaimed, "There

Is No Death!"

She went on, "We who are blessed (or cursed, depending on your view) can help those like yourself to learn something about it. Tell me, what gave you the idea of coming here tonight?" Alice said she wasn't sure, but she thought it might have been a dream she had the other night. She said she had no intention of coming here, but well, here she was! "That's interesting," the medium looked thoughtful for a moment. "As a matter of fact, the man I came to with his wife said much the same thing. Something told him to come, too. His wife died of cancer about six weeks ago, and the poor man has missed her very badly. He and you, too, I would say, have been told to come so that his wife, and your son, could get their messages across to you, through me. Don't look so surprised! It happens all the time, here!"

Alice White went home that night in a warm glow. She had been through an experience she would not have thought possible. Even now, she still found it hard to believe. But the evidence was there, and the lady, Violet, could not possibly have known anything: about her or her son. So, it had to have come from Arthur, taken from her at the very start of his adult life. Was there a God? She didn't know. Was there really life after death? There had to be, considering this experience, but how? She had been reading something not long ago about reincarnation, spirits, and such things, but the writer seemed to do everything possible to destroy such ideas. He seemed to have very little idea about any God as well. So, what was the truth?

She could not refute that she had to take it further. She did something she would never have dreamt she would ever do; she became involved in the organisation, which had unexpectedly opened up a future beyond her wildest imagination.

Snow, while still miffed at not being able to talk to his mother directly, was nevertheless thrilled with the evening's work. He had believed, as many do, that these mediums were all a load of bunk, con artists out for a quick dollar. Sean pointed out that there were still a few like that, but very few, for none of those ever stood up to any scrutiny, and the genuine outstripped the frauds so far that they had virtually ceased to exist. Snow shook his head at this further example of the intransigence of the so-called experts at putting down something being experienced by thousands all over the world.

He further wondered at the impossibility of ever convincing another, more so if he were a sceptic, of any purely subjective experience, such as he knew his mother had just had. The sceptic would, of course, rubbish such a thing, merely a figment of an overworked imagination. Too much gin! Sean, as usual, was quite up to guidance, which, if not explaining it all, directed the person to consider some other aspect of the question.

"All you need to do," he beamed, "Is to think, 'If it's true for you, then it's true. If it isn't true for you, it isn't true,' that's all!"

"So, if you experience something you cannot share with someone else, how the hell do you know whether you're not dreaming? Just hallucinating? How the hell can you tell?" Paul seemed to be the one who always came up with the awkward question,

"You can't tell," Sean gave a little grimace, "If you're the only one experiencing something, you must decide whether to accept it or not. It's only when you can share it, will it become real."

"Do you mean by that, that a thought I have, or that you have, is just that unless someone else agrees about it?" Paul persisted. Sean nodded.

"What is reality then? What is real if it all seems to start out as someone's thoughts?"

Sean muttered, "Nothing much the matter with your mind! You're quick! I can answer with one word. In fact, you just said it. Agreement. That is all" He grimaced again and spread his hands, "Agreement. When two or more agree about something, it then becomes real to them, and the more that agree about it - whatever it may be – the more solid and substantial it becomes."

Paul shook his head in wonder. He made a face at the torrent of new ideas pouring down upon him; he knew he had asked for it, with his interminable questions. There was so much to try to soak up. At the same time, he was now fully aware of the danger of merely swallowing all this whole, accepting it simply because it came from what seemed an impeccable source. He knew now that Man knows nothing just by being told it; it was necessary for him to actually experience it, taste it, and live it.

He felt the need to get away for a while, do something different, something which might allow him to explore those parts of the realms open to him. He wanted to include Jane in his plans but was intrigued to discover that she and Snow, his new-found companion of earthly days, were siblings; he was the brother she had lost many years before, when she was quite young. They had a great deal to fill in, having been separated by almost two lifetimes.

Both she and Snow were so delighted by this discovery that they were lost to all others for some little time, leaving Paul at a loose end.

He decided to take Sean's advice and take a little holiday. But where would he go? Another trip to the lower regions made him shudder, despite knowing he could come to no harm. There must be somewhere he could go, somewhere of interest. As he looked about, he thought he could see a range of high hills, perhaps even mountains, blue and faint in the distance. Could he go that far? Sean, as usual, not very far off, sauntered over.

"Well, what's stopping you? You're a free man. Go where you will! Just take off!"

"But...do I walk? Or is there some other way? I don't want to just arrive there - I want to see what's along the way..."

Sean looked at him, a little smile on his round face. "Remember, this is a world of Thought! Whatever you think; is so! And as you also know by now or should do is qualified by one thing; your certainty that what you think, is so. Just as you created the thought, so it is."
"So, me lad, if you want to fly, then fly!"

Walkabout

He was flying, just like his dreams. Exactly like the dreams, only more so, if that were possible. The dreams allowed him to just push himself up, with a gigantic leap, and go up, up, and away.

So, he did that, but now with the certainty of success, in the mind-boggling simplicity of all things here, in these realms of the living dead. "No!" he corrected himself sternly, "Not the dead! I cannot accept that I'm dead, but I know that I died. So, I must accept what all these teachers say - I cannot die."

Yet he had the greatest difficulty in knowing that he was not dreaming. This was real! As he soared effortlessly up, moving in the first direction that occurred to him, he slowly relaxed. Once, in a heart-stopping swoop down towards the fields below, he soon discovered how easy it was to recover his nerve. His height, his progress, and his peace of mind. Just thought.

"That's far enough!" was enough. With a growing feeling of intense delight, he found complete freedom high above the cultivated fields below. He soared, swooped, and soared again in the fulfilment of the age-old dream of flying, really flying, with the advantage of never failing again. Now he could explore with the advantage of height.

But what, he thought, were these cultivated fields doing in this place? Was this not a spiritual realm? Was it necessary to grow crops here, to feed hungry hordes? There were little settlements here and there, exactly as one might find anywhere on Earth, with paths, streams, trees, and people, everywhere. He came down closer for a better look, to find out something about them - who they were, and why they were here. He felt an insatiable urge to know more and more about this fascinating place.

This started a tour which took him far and wide, over to, and beyond the mountains well-populated as he saw. There was little sign of the crude ramshackle hovels he had seen on his earlier journeying. He saw well-kept houses, gardens, and well-dressed people.

This was so like the Earth he had known, that if he were not flying, he would be hard-pressed to know the difference. That, along with the never-changing light - he still had no idea as to its source, and the wide differences in building styles he saw scattered about made it much easier to accept. Included in that was the wide variety of clothing styles he encountered, even one with none at all, in one field he passed over.

One thing struck him. He was the only one flying. He saw no others, and by the commotion, he caused as he cruised along at about fifty feet up, he was a rarity. It was worth investigating.

There were about six or seven men and women working in a garden, so he drifted down, coming to a halt six feet or so up, not sure of his reception. They all saw him and came over slowly, ready to run. They stopped at what they thought was a safe distance. One man asked nervously, "Where you from? How come you-all stays up in the air like that'n?"

"Just over the way a bit," he pointed casually, "No need to be afraid - I just want to talk. I'm just out visiting, getting to know this country. What's it called?" "Can't say as I rightly knows! We ain't got a name that I knows of, seein' as how all the land hereabouts is pretty-much the same, like; it don't rain, but everything grows like it did where we come from."

Paul slowly drifted down to the group and stood before them, knowing there was no malice or anything to fear. Just curiosity. There was no need to ask their origin - it was obvious. They were farmers, all from the mid-western USA, good, kindly people, not easily upset by trivia, ready to meet good or bad, fire, flood, or famine with the courage of their forefathers. He was to meet many similar groups in his wanderings.

After a few visits like that, he saw what was keeping them in that situation. This was the very common refusal to accept that they were in the realms of spiritual life, that they had passed through that dreaded portal feared by so many and were no longer Earth-bound. Also, their Bible-belt origin led them to believe in Peter at the Gate, Golden streets, angels, harps, and God on His throne passing out judgement. As the reality was not at all like the expectation, they could not be dead, and they all still had a long way to go. This land was exactly like home, even to the Pastor going on about Hell and Damnation. Their churches and pastors were also here.

So, it was quite natural for them to set up the same communities at home, complete with all the restricted viewpoints. Paul, however, had changed since his arrival from a selfish egocentric, wrapped up in his own bigotry that made him shudder now at the memory of it. He realised now, that for all the authoritative views accepted by these simple folk, how much worse off they would be without any; they would be no better off than that bunch at Jack the Giants village.

A little farther on, he met a similar group, this time from South-West England, with exactly the same outlook as the Americans, for the same reasons and the same results. If he had approached this little safari with the intention of bringing any of these folk to some understanding of where and what they were, he would have gone home empty-handed. They were all very contented. He wondered what it might take to shake them out of their complacency; the act of dying certainly had not, despite being met on arrival as Paul had, and could not believe it.

On and on he went, over this peaceful land, with little change evident. It seemed to go on and on forever, and he was starting: to understand just how mind-bogglingly huge these realms were. He also wondered if, because of the sameness, the lack of pressure, or demands of any kind, they were not bored to death. But no, they were not. At least those few he spoke to assured him there was plenty to do. There were village fairs, fetes, picnics, competitions, concerts, and all manner of things to do. So, whatever they may be, they were not apathetic. Just strangely incurious about their state of existence and environment.

Then, he struck up a friendship with a small group who were not afraid to talk openly without any fear of wrath from their leaders. It appeared that most of these people - and there were a multitude of them who were actually afraid of asking any awkward questions for fear of losing what was literally, a slice of Heaven.

No Taxmen, no debts, no robberies, no rapes, no bitter cold, snow, floods. Just - well, just Heaven.

So, whatever you do, don't rock the boat! Don't look this gift-horse in the mouth. Almighty God has seen fit to reward us; we know not why or for how long. So, we gratefully accept, but no questions, please!

One thing did bother many of them. There were no Bibles. They had asked, searched, and asked again and again, but no Bibles could be found. Then he discovered this handful of people living in a less salubrious state, although they were happy enough. It turned out that they had been banished. Exiled. Just because they dared challenge their pastor on his teachings about Heaven and Hell.

There were five in the group, three girls and two men, all Anglo-Saxon in origin, and while they had some contact with Christian teaching, it was quite superficial: something very common with these people. But the transition from the physical realm to this had not gone un-noticed, and much discussion, some fairly heated, had brought the conclusion that something had happened and that something was unexpected.

They had died, in the understanding of Earth-bound humanity, but they were not dead. This caused them to question their good pastor, who took umbrage - as seemed so common here among these folk. He called them troublemakers and told them either to conform or leave. They knew they were not dead. So, they left, with great pleasure.

So, here they were, more confused than ever. Their endless arguing was all centred around what little background they had on religious matters, religion being synonymous with Christianity, there being no other - also, a universal belief. This, of course, covered such things as Hell, Devil, Heaven, reward, forgiveness, and all those ideas which, without any thought, made up what was accepted as a 'Faith.'

They had reluctantly been drawn to the conclusion that the Spiritualist movement was right in their assertion that there is no death. Hence their discomfort, for this door is firmly closed by almost all Christian churches, by virtue of the Bible, in Deuteronomy, chapter eighteen, verses ten to twelve.

But the broadest thinker of this group had studied a little more than his friends, and in particular, the Book in question. He had been amazed to read the strangely conflicting statements therein. This seemed to be an expansion of the Commandments and seemed to ramble a bit.

For instance, he said, 'Thou shalt not kill.' Then a page or two later, 'thou shall have no other Gods before me.' Then it went on that if any man or woman was found to worship some other God, you must take them out and stone them to death! They wondered how this could be claimed to be the Word of God! So, they were glad to be on their own and go it alone.

And, as Paul could see, they were doing very well. The one who had won the discussion on their true situation had naturally gravitated to being a leader, and it was he who Paul approached. Paul had been attracted by the difference in the house he saw below; it was made of a framework covered with a roof of reeds, thatch-style, gathered from a nearby lake. A little curious, for the buildings he had seen to date were solidly constructed, built he knew not how or with what materials, but solidly and neatly. It seemed someone had arranged for them to be there, and there they were!

One might turn around and find a cottage where there was none. Usually, this was accepted with a shrug and the thought that "I must have missed something when I first looked. Houses don't just appear! If I thought that, I'd be nuts!"

So, Paul drifted down and settled before the surprised man. "Hello!" he said cheerfully, "My name is Paul Askew. I come in peace and friendship!" He extended his hand. The man gripped it, "Glad to meet you! At last, someone sounds sensible around here. I'm Johann, and I come from Holland."

By this time, the others had arrived and were introduced. He tried to remember their names; there were Liz, Di, Jo, and Ben. They crowded around, all interested in his dress and how he managed to arrive by air. Paul laughed, "Easy! You just fly!" He gave a big grin and lifted a few inches off the ground, "As easy as that. But tell me, why are you by yourselves away out here?"

"Oh," Johann grinned wryly. "We didn't like being told what to believe. So, we moved out. We were told we were damned, doomed, and otherwise lost. But where did you come from?"

"A little village over that way," he pointed, "There, nobody tells us what to believe, or what to think, or what not to think. We are very lucky to have a very good teacher. But tell me, do you know you're in the land of spiritual existence?" They all tried to speak at once. A jumble of thoughts made it rather difficult to understand, but Paul got the gist of it, "That's one thing we're sure of, because we were all together!" Johann went on, "We're dead alright, except we are not, and that's a puzzle! We all died together, for we were all on the same plane when it crashed, and we all got converted to pulp. But look at us! No pulp! All in one piece. So, what are we? We must be ghosts… or… what?"

Paul replied, "You are just basically you, and that is a being, capable of thought, independent action, and basically a spirit; you are all individuals, all separate, even unique. There is only one like you, and that is you. No other is exactly like you because each of you - me too - is the sum of all our experiences, good, bad, and indifferent. For all that, we are all a part of the Great White Spirit, of Almighty God, with all the attributes and abilities of God; in fact, we are all gods in the making."

The little group looked from one to the other and looked back at

Paul, all a little bemused. Then Ben spoke up, "That's a bit sweeping, isn't it? I mean, aren't we being a bit, well, er, arrogant? How can we claim such a privileged place in, er, the hierarchy?" Paul gave a little grin, unaware that he was copying Sean, "Did you see me fly?" They all nodded doubtfully.

"Anyone can fly!" He spread his arms. Johann still looked doubtful. "If you can do that, you can walk on water too! Does that mean you can work miracles? Are you as good as Jesus Christ?" They all started talking at once. He let them go for a moment, then held up his hands.

"I should be able to walk on water if I can fly but realise that is only in this realm! I cannot do these things on Earth, or could not, while I was there. But wait! You must be prepared, as I had to learn, to chuck away all your preconceived ideas. Throw them out the window. I see now that you've already started to do that, while all the others you left when coming out here remain stuck in prisons of their own making because they cannot accept any new ideas."

"If you want, you will learn that one thing Jesus, the Nazarene, said to his followers many times, 'What I am, any man can be! What I do, any man can do.' These words are found in the Book of God's Remembrance, available to any who desire higher studies."

One thing Paul didn't want was to sound like a pedantic professor; he had to liven it up a bit. "So, you all croaked - kicked the bucket! And yet you live here. And this ain't no Merry England or the land of windmills! As the Man said, and I guess you know this one, 'In my Father's house, there are many mansions.' This is only one of them!"

"What are they like, these other mansions?" demanded the group. "Are they anything like this?"

"Much better, and also, a hell of a lot worse!" Paul said a little ruefully, "I know from personal experience about the worse ones! I've been there! I know!" he scowled with distaste. He was immediately assailed with demands to tell them all about it. So, he did, and as he spoke, he found two unexpected things; the memories of Billy the Bully and his merry men became much easier to look at, just by talking about it, and secondly, he found a natural gift for story-telling, and from that grew a pleasure in teaching which was to become his main occupation. As he finished, Jo said thoughtfully, "So, what keeps us here, and them, there, is it just what view they have of themselves, and ourselves too. Is that right? And the ones you met sounded like proper tearaways - like that Jack, was that him? They stay there because of the way they treat others, right? That means…" she answered her own question, "They must all be the types that don't care! Thieves and rogues!"

Paul started to speak, but Ben got in first, "But isn't there someone in charge of them? You can't allow bruisers like that loose on the landscape? That's why we have prisons!" For all Paul had been able to learn, there were still many gaps yet to be filled, but he knew Sean could fill them. And blow me down! Just the thought was enough! There he was! Wonderful old Sean!

"Hey! Hey! Not so much of the Old, young Paul! Introduce me to your friends." In a dream-like atmosphere of surprise and wonder, along with the almost blasé notion that this happens all the time here, they all shook hands with Sean, who beamed paternally at them. The introductions over, he turned to Ben, "Now, since you ask, I shall tell you."

"In the entire Cosmos, nothing happens unnoticed and unrecorded. And while none of us, from the Highest Masters down to the lowliest teachers like Paul here, and myself, can interfere with the freedom of any individual, there are other means of ensuring that no harm can be done by any person to any other person, particularly on the lower levels. Here, usually, no harm is ever done to another. Lower, attempted harm is the norm."

"For any of us - including those lower - our strength, both physical and spiritual, is always a measure of our consciousness, our spiritual awareness. The less aware a person is, the less able they are to work with others. Someone may be a highly qualified, respected leader on Earth; upon arrival here, if he is dead spiritually, he will have very little life force here. He will probably attempt to carry on as before, the big boss ordering others about. And, of course, if he were a criminal, he would try to do exactly as he did before."

"Of course, if he were dead spiritually, he would be the closest to the living dead you will find here. To the ones around them, they would seem quite normal, as it is normal to them. They do not know this difference. Poor wretches, for they are all the same mind, ignorant, and not knowing they are ignorant. Compared to you, they are in hell."

"Yes, but," Ben argued, "On Earth, they can do untold harm to others."

"Ah yes, you're quite right," Sean agreed. "And that is because Earth-Plane life is where you grow, develop, and balance your karma, and if you are not very careful and take the trouble to learn a little about it, you will incur more debt to settle, somewhere, sometime, but settled it must be."

"Here, everything depends on your spiritual worth – or lack of it – and while progress is available to all who may learn as fast and as much as they desire, those others who remain dead spiritually, remain exactly where they are with a corresponding ineffectiveness against others."

"I, myself, regretfully must soon leave this realm to return to Earth, to work off some of my own debts – they go back quite a way, unfortunately." He sighed, grinned ruefully, and sat down, fully aware that they expected him to enlarge on that. He continued, "I was a priest on Earth, and I believe, a good one; I kept all my vows. I was careful and conscientious. But oh my! Along with all religious beliefs, I was doing the right thing. The teachings were noble, grand even, and sonorously eloquent, calculated to sweep one off one's feet without the vitally necessary opportunity of allowing us to attempt to question what they insisted was the truth!"

"As you will learn – if you have the desire to do so- the Master Jesus said that you know nothing by simply being told it is so. Knowledge, true knowledge is gained only one way, direct experience."

"But the hierarchy in my church allowed us none of that sort of freedom! We accepted what was given us without question, and precious few permitted. And, of course, thus extended to our own preaching, as we did what was demanded of us."

"In turn, we insisted our flocks accepted just as blindly, whatever we said. The doubters were always told that they must have Faith, and any who could not accept that, were unbelievers, heretics, even."

"Now, God help me! I told many lies, although I didn't know they were. And further, I ruined many innocent lives by forcing the doctrines of the church. You see, I was a priest in several lifetimes, several incarnations. This covered the period of the inquisitions, the

Auto Da Fe, the most brutal period in history. Few escaped their attention, and if one fell into their hands, he would be very lucky to escape untouched."

"I'm afraid to say it, but I must. The Mother Church has failed its purpose. Abysmally failed. Instead of bringing souls to the God-light, they produced slaves, and then, to further their exalted position, decked themselves in finery, in costly raiment's, resided in palaces, and lived off the fat of the land, provided by an impoverished populace."

"Is it any wonder Luther broke away from the Mother Church, seeking true enlightenment? Unfortunately, this started a whole series of breakaway movements, all claiming to peddle the truth, using as their basis, an already discredited dogma, creed, et cetera."

"And you no doubt know, many of these breakaway groups are so wrapped up in their righteousness that they are willing to kill each other to prove, themselves right! Oh, my."

"Do you mean that the whole of Christianity is just hot air? Is the original story about this man Jesus all rubbish?" Johann was very confused by all this. He knew, because of the inherent nature of thought, that few things remained hidden, so he knew that Sean was sincere. But of course, this upset all of his early understanding of Christianity on the level in which most people have come into contact, either through parents, schools or perhaps direct contact with a church.

"Oh no, dear me, no!" Sean hastened to reply, "Jesus was a master soul. There had been masters before him, and there will be masters to come. Oh, dear me, no, he lived and was a master. If you wish, you may study the true teachings of these masters, and you will learn that what they taught varies very little, from master to master. Their message has always been to love thy neighbour, do unto others as you would have them do unto you, all those things I am sure you already know."

"In every case, a priesthood soon sprang up around such teachings. The disciples of the masters did their best to follow his lead, made some alterations to what was told to them, mostly through simple misinterpretation. Take a good look at the work and teachings of Saul of Tarsus, who, while never meeting Jesus, took upon himself the leadership of the others and soon became their Authority, bigoted as he was. And then the priests got into the act and further adulterated the original teachings, becoming The Authority."

"Jesus, Gautama Siddhartha whom you may know as Buddha, Osiris and the others had no desire to found religions; they merely wished to bring a state of enlightenment, to get them to understand their position with God and the actions which would raise their consciousness, their spirituality. None of these ideas put forward, contained any orders. The priests to come brought that in, to make their positions more secure, as much as anything. They also brought in punishment for back-sliders, those judged to be heretics, or any others who dared to question their doctrines."

Johann let out a huge sigh. "Thank God I've at last met someone who could explain all this. At last, it starts to make some real sense!"

"That's fine," Ben spoke up, "But how can we tell the truth from the fiction? The wheat from the chaff? How can ordinary people like us find out?" He looked around at the others with a little frown. "We've always been told, for instance, that Jesus died so that our sins would be forgiven. He was crucified to take away our sins. Is that true?"

"No, it is not," Sean replied with his little wry smile, "I had always believed that, of course, along with countless others. But the Master Jesus said, many times - and you will not find this in your King James Version – that no man can pay for another's deeds or misdeeds. Only the doer, the one who did it, can put it right. This is Cosmic Law, God's Law, Karmic Law. It cannot be changed or ignored, and cannot fail. One may spend many lifetimes working at putting right whatever he did that was wrong. I believe you had a man in Germany recently who was responsible for some horrendous things. I expect he will be spending a very long time correcting his misdeeds."

"Of course, if he chooses, he need not do anything; he may stay as he is but believe me, he will stay. And he will not be very comfortable. Paul has seen what it can be like for such as him. It's their choice entirely. They run one important risk, however. If they stay there, they may be led, encouraged even, to deny the existence of the Supreme Being of this Cosmos. This is the one sure way to bring about their non-existence. Since we - all of us, good and bad - are part of God, Gods in the making: to deny God is to deny oneself. That, and that alone, will bring about permanent demise. Wipe-out, I believe Paul's generation would say."

"So, why was the statement 'God so loved the World that He gave his only begotten son that who-soever believeth in Him shall not perish but have everlasting life.' to give the full statement. Why?"

"If you have made even a cursory study of the early religions of Earth, you will have seen that it was necessary to placate whatever god there was, in order to be saved from disaster, or to have a good harvest or any other like reason. This was a mainstay of the old Judaic faith and persisted until well after the murder of Jesus. Then, taken as part of the new faith, it was still necessary to make sacrifice to God. This soon became doctrine, Holy Writ!"

"Jesus, on more than one occasion, chided the priests for the awful stench of burning flesh on their altars. He told them it was an affront to God, as indeed it is. And priests being priests, these things soon became enforceable. To this day, this is accepted as the reason for the terrible deed committed against Jesus."

"Now, I expect you have many more questions, but as my young friend Paul found out, the answers are available to any who seek." They all started talking at once. Sean looked at Paul with his little smile. Paul gave a little grimace, more than a smile in reply. He knew he had acted exactly the same way on having a few gems of enlightenment cast before him; He had to admit that while he had made good progress, he had some way to go; much of what Sean had just said was new to him, but with a little thought he was able to add to what he had already absorbed and digested. Sean nodded knowingly.

"Yes, me lad! If you continue to keep your eyes and ears open, you will go a long way! But now, after satisfying your curiosity in stopping off here - and doing a good job for them, incidentally - you should continue your little tour. When you return, there is something I want to show you." Paul pricked up his ears and leaned forward eagerly.

"No, no, not yet! Wait until you come back! Just now, you head over to that mountain range and poke your nose over the top; you might be surprised!" Sean waved him away and busied himself with the little group, inviting them to join the others at what Paul, for want of something better, called Seanville.

So, what was on the other side of the mountain? He could have just gone there flick, flick, but he chose to drift along, although faster than before. He kept thinking about the bear that went over the mountain to see what he could see, and the song ran out as he saw the other side.

Sean was right, of course. He was surprised! The last thing he expected to see was this great ocean! He looked in amazement. There were boats, yachts, dinghies, and even larger vessels he thought might be schooners, but he knew little about marine things. There were also some ships with no visible means of propulsion; did they have engines? He snorted to himself, "What a damn silly idea!" but he had to ask.

"No, of course not!" the man laughed, "What do you think this is? Heaven?"

"Well, what makes them go, then?"

"We do! We just think they move along, and away they go. When we want some real speed, we join forces, two or three of us. Then we really Humm along! Even have races." Paul shrugged with this new proof that this was indeed the realm of Thought.

And there was more to see than just see pretty little coves, boats, and such: the whole area was more heavily populated than he had seen. He wondered if this was due to just being in a nice place. Everything was neat, clean, and well-kept. Ah yes! Simple! These people were more spiritually conscious than any he had yet met.

He was curious to know what these folk thought – what they knew. A good opportunity arose alongside a little cove, where two men sat enjoying the peaceful scene. He walked over to them. "Mind if I sit down?" The men nodded companionably, and one of them replied, "Help yourself. You from these parts?"

"No," Paul sat where the man tapped the wall beside him, "I'm from over the hill," he pointed, "Just taking a look around. Lovely little place you have here!" The one who had spoken grunted, "Yup! We like it. I been 'ere - oh, I dunno – I've forgot when I came 'ere. We's old fisher-folk from oh, 'way back. We comes 'ere all the time, us does."

"Do you know how you come to be here? Did something happen to you?" The man laughed a contented soft chuckle. "He he! Oh, we knows, right enough! Him and me was out fishin'. We 'ad a full catch on board too. But we stayed out too long·. That channel will al-us get you! He he! Got us both; it did! We was trying to turn to run before it but as we started t' turn, the fish slipped to starb'd, and we rolled straight over. It all happened so darn quick it was all over in a flash, and 'ere we was, flounderin' around, and our boat gone. Sank like a bloody stone! And us silly buggers, neither of us could swim, not that it would do any good, seein' as we was six miles out! So, we went to Davey Jones' locker! Except we finished up 'ere!

"So, we have to be dead! And talkin' to a feller we met, he sez so. An' 'e told us what we are - said this is our proper selves! Fancy that! I dunno what he meant by that, but it's sure good 'ere. Good mates, a swig o' rum now and then. Only thing, a few of the fellers that come ere want us to go to school! Ha! Ha! School? At our time o' life!" He punched his friend on the shoulder and they both laughed heartily. Eventually the speaker calmed down and continued, "Yes, well, me mum - she lives just up the street - she was one of these clare-something or other- I never get it right - and she says this is a sort of heaven, and we're here in this place 'cause we – that's Allister and me - are ordinary fellers- not bad, seein' we got a decent respect for the law, that's what they say -wot he meant, but he reckons there's places 'ere hardly fit for pigs, and the ones wot go there are the real bad 'uns - like, thieves and murderers, and they stay there cause they can't see this place. Is that right? Is that the same as they tell you?"

"That's right!" Paul agreed, "I've been there - I know! All the villains go there! He gave the men an outline of his travels, and they looked at each other and back to Paul in disbelief. This developed into an invitation to stay with them; a mutual attraction had grown between them. Paul admired their forthright honesty and for all their lack of formal education, were astute judges of character, acquired by many years of associating with good, bad, and ornery! They knew the value of trust and loyal, brave companions. This placed them immeasurably above those unfortunates.

These people were civilised! This came as a sudden shock stopping him in his tracks. They were civilised! And just as suddenly, he realised that up to then, there had never been true civilisation at anytime, anywhere, on Planet Earth! Certainly, not in this present era. Earlier, he was not sure: he was lacking data there, but most certainly, this era had never known civilisation! The true definition of the word was staring him in the face. 'Civilised.' Or perhaps ' Technologised,' that was all. Barbarians with nylon stockings, fast cars, enormous, high buildings, jet aircraft, and the means of instant and total wipe-out! But nowhere over the face of the planet, was there other than a handful of people here and there who were willing - nay - dedicated, to solving their problems and difficulties by means other than the use of force.

Violence was more often the first action to settle a difference or to take something not one's own. And he had to come here, to the realms of Spirit, to find an entire community living by peaceful means, without coercion. Not a cop in sight! There were none!

He would have been very happy to stay there. The atmosphere was so pleasant, and it was a very beautiful place, nestled in a wide valley with the mountain peak at its head. Neat houses, trees, gardens, all in rich confusion, spread out over the valley down to the harbour, where the many craft were moored with still more moving about.

But he felt he really must be getting back to Jane, Sean, and the others, particularly when he recalled Sean saying that he had something to show him.

This time he went back by the direct route; he built up a little picture of the little village, and there he was. But he found he was a bit miffed by the casual reception he got. He didn't want a brass band, but, well, some enthusiasm would have been nice. Jane welcomed him as if he had not been away, but according to his subjective time sense, he had been away, oh, maybe, two or three weeks.

This was another facet of life here, this vexing question of Time. How was it possible for someone to experience a very different timescale from oneself? And what the hell is Time, anyway? He knew nobody here was regulated by that implacable thing, as solid and unvarying as the Earth, utterly dependable, and just as utterly controlling. Yet here, there were no timepieces, no such thing as 'Dinner at six' and 'Concert at eight.'

For once, it was not Sean who explained to Paul - along with others just as interested - it was John. "In the physical universe, Time is one of the basic factors, along with matter, energy, and space."

"Matter is actually energy that has become a little more solid than the energy of, say, pure thought, which of course, is energy too. The more agreement you get on your thought-created energy, the more solid it becomes. You know very well how this works in the physical Universe! Everyone is in full agreement about how solid the universe is. It is very solid. Have you ever tried to walk through a wall?"

"So, energy is where the matter originates. This is one of those things that you find becoming much clearer as you go on. Space is a concept that there is something between thee and me. That 'something' is quite important, because if we could not establish that-er-thing, however small, between us, and whatever we wish to see, we could not perceive it."

"So, we invent Space. It allows things to happen. No space, nothing can move, act, react, just nothing."

"Now, Time is the concept which explains to us on the physical plane, that something has changed. There, as the sun changes position minute by minute, hour by hour, at a predictable rate, we say time has passed, this being reinforced by clocks. If nothing at all changed, we would get the idea that time is standing still."

"Now, here in this realm, since we have neither night or day or clocks, our time sense gets less and less as we stay here and is now the direct result of what we are doing."

"Paul went off to have a look around. He was busy looking, talking, learning, too, I'll bet. A certain time was experienced subjectively by him while he was away. Us lot here have been doing not much nor moving about. So, to us, not much has happened, so not much time has gone by. And that, my friends, is that."

"Ok," thought Paul, "But that, as usual, raises more questions. We have all these things here; matter," He looked at the solid-looking trees, houses, and people. "Energy - explains itself, as it seems. Life itself is energy, and we have space, as you have just said. Time, well, I guess I go along with that as well. So, if we have all these things here, why is this not a physical universe, like the one we came from?"

John looked at him, an understanding gleam in his eye. "Not so difficult, really. First, that matter here is invisible on Earth because it is much finer in texture and is away outside the range of human vision. Then, the energy we have here is universal, and if you got yourself really wound up, the things you could do would surprise you! The other things, space and time, are the same anywhere, Earth, Mars, or here. And don't forget that everything is just as solid as there is agreement about it."

"Another thing, On Earth, if you go around disagreeing with others on what they accept as real, you'll get locked up! Here, you can please yourself. As you become more aware of yourselves, your own beingness, you can please yourself whether you agree with anyone or not. Your freedom."

Re-union

Paul stood in speechless wonder. Surrounded by unimagined beauty he slowly turned, in an effort to take it all in. They were standing on a promontory overlooking what had to be Emerald City, spread out below them. Sean, a huge grin on his face, spread his hands expansively.

"Well?" he asked, eyebrows raised.

"You mean, we just came here? We just - just walked in! After the trouble, we had the last time we tried."

"Yes," Sean, still grinning, "I knew you were ready when you came back with your friend..." "But" Paul interrupted, "How? I feel the same as I did before – you know - when Jane and I tried..." He was slightly embarrassed, as if he had just gate-crashed a VIP party, but with Sean at his side, calm and confident, he began to relax a little, although he was still at a loss at what he regarded as a promotion being achieved so easily.

"But...But I've done nothing. What could I have done to make it so easy?"

It had been easy too. Sean had said, "Come along! I want to show you something." He took his arm, and they set off along a barely outlined path. It happened without any warning whatever, leaving him shocked with surprise and disbelief. They had burst out, like a train charging out of a tunnel, into the tranquil beauty of this, the realm of the Blessed Spirits, the name Paul in his imaginings had bestowed on it.

"No, lad, not quite that! Oh, I know the legend. Orpheus visits the underworld on his way to the Blessed Spirits looking for his love, Euridice. No, this is the realm to which any soul who has provided selfless service to others is most likely to come."

"Don't get me wrong, now! This is not regarded as a reward. If someone were to set out, for instance, to pile up credits to pay their way, they would be disappointed, and there are many, like myself, believing they have well and truly earned a place here - priests, clerics and the like - get an unpleasant surprise!" The look on Sean's face showed that he had been one of them.

"Do ye mean you couldn't come here? Just like us?" Paul asked in puzzlement.

"I do mean that; indeed, I do! I was knocked flat by the company I was in! And I had the devil of a job unlearning all the things which I had mistakenly taught to so many. Oh, yes, it was very difficult. But I was lucky. I had some good tutors, and I was able to develop. The most important thing I had to learn was humility! That, and the realisation that there were many - oh, a great many - worse off than myself. So, I was given the chance to help many of these, and I was also to learn that this was the best way to help one's self."

"Now, what did you think about that place you visited; the place over the mountain?"

Paul looked at him wondering at the sudden change in subject. Answering cautiously, he said, "Very nice, I thought; a beautiful place, and some very nice people..." He came to a halt, wondering at the real intent of the question. Sean laughed.

"Yes, I was hoping you would go there. So, it was alright, was it?" Paul bridled a little as he tried to see the drift. What was he supposed to see, or feel? Sean stood, an expectant air about him. This made Paul look back at his visit, seeing again the little cove and the two fishermen he had met, and found an immediate change of scene. They were in the little cove, with the two fishermen smiling at them.

"Who's your friend, Paul?" In a little fog of confusion, he introduced Sean to the two men, who stood up declaring, "This calls for a celebration! Let's go to the Admiral Benbow!"

They had only a few yards to go along the waterfront to the lovely little inn nestled in behind the harbour wall. Paul could not help comparing this with the last tavern he had visited. These folk were civil, and therefore civilised. There was a cheerful fire in the huge grate – not necessary, because it was not cold - but it added to the cozy atmosphere. Tables, chairs, the inevitable dart board, boxes of dominoes, a lovely ornate bar with many colourful bottles on the shelves. The customers were all friendly, neatly dressed, with a relaxed air of happiness and pleasure in shared company, while the barman, cheerful and smiling, had a marvellous handle-bar moustache.

Somehow, Paul had missed this on his previous visit, but then, he had not stayed long. He was quite taken by it; a true smugglers den with all the trimmings but one - there were characters, but no villains.

Sean put a pint-pot in his hand and led him to a table at which the fishermen were already seated, lounging back expansively as they exchanged greetings with others already happily engaged in the ancient pastime of supping a jug of good ale, in good company.

But while Paul was enjoying himself - the ale was a rich brown brew, very good - something about the name of the inn pecked away at his memory. It was very familiar, but probably just another of those delightful English places he had heard about.

Sean thumped his empty tankard on the table, "I thought you might like to visit your friends, and perhaps meet a very old one." He had a huge grin on his face.

"Who do you mean?" Paul frowned a little, "Who would I know here - other than Dan and Allister here?"

"Ah! Here he comes now, I think."

A tall man with sparse hair and deep melancholic eyes entered and said in a soft Scottish brogue, "Usual, please, Alfred!" He took a coin from his Victorian westkit pocket and looked around, nodding to those present. "Certainly, Mr. Stevenson." He placed a whiskey glass before him and neatly poured a generous snort.

Paul watched as he turned, and seeing an empty chair beside him he approached as Paul stared in speechless awe. Of course! The Admiral Benbow! And the great man himself asking for permission to sit with them! Unbelieving, he was sharing a table with the great Robert Louis Stevenson.

And, as usual, Sean was quite right; he was an old boyhood friend. He well remembered the forbidden pleasure in reading in bed, after lights out, of the wonderful voyage to Treasure Island and all that happened there, blankets over his head to conceal the little flashlight.

The great man soon had Paul relaxed and enjoying the company of one so illustrious but with a gentlemanly modesty, Paul could only warm to. He soon drew Paul out and listened with interest as Paul told his simple story, finishing with,

"But you don't want to hear about me." He shrugged, slightly embarrassed, "I'm nobody!"

"Oh, but I do! I'm learning all I can about different people; I find them fascinating. And you come from another culture; an interesting one. We often heard about New Zealand in Samoa, And I met several from your country there. Very practical people." He broke off abruptly and stared into space for a few moments. Then he gave a little start and turned to the others.

"Forgive me, I was thinking about Samoa, and wishing I knew as much then as I know now when I wrote that little thing! I was quite certain I would spend eternity under that wide and starry sky. Here I am, and damn glad to be here!"

That was the beginning of many enjoyable sessions with the man, who had undoubtedly earned the title of Tusitala. He told many a tale, mostly apocryphal, and many bawdy ones as well.

And while their relationship grew to firm friendship, another encounter brought the full realisation of what had happened, unobtrusively and unnoticed.

After one of the many yarn-spinning sessions, the party had broken up to go their various ways, with an agreement to meet again soon. Paul stood enjoying the tranquil scene, savouring the many laughs he had just shared with the real prince of story tellers, when two young ladies came along. He paid them little attention, at first. But something about one of them made him look again.

"Hey," he thought "she walks and talks like Moira!" As she grew closer, his heart gave a huge leap. It was Moira. Chatting away to her companion, she was about to pass Paul, when she looked at him. For a brief moment she frowned, trying to put a name to the familiar but strange man before her. Then, with a cry of surprise she clutched his arm.

"Paul! Paul! It IS you! What…how… Oh! It's lovely to see you here! What happened? The last time I saw you…" She kissed him, "was back in that nice little village. Oh it's good to see you," she repeated. "What brings you here? "Remember you couldn't come here before."

Paul looked from one to the other of the women in utter surprise, thinking that Moira must have come visiting him again. But her words started to sink in as he realised, she was wondering what it was that brought him here. That meant – slow realisation lit his face. The full impact of his presence hit them both at once.

"Paul! Oh Paul, I am so glad." She flung her arms around his neck. "You must tell me how! You've changed!" She broke away abruptly, reaching out to her companion, she brought her forward.

"Oh. Forgive me Jo," she turned back to Paul. "This is Josephine Forbes-Hamilton" and then to her she said "Paul and I were engaged back on Earth. Now, I don't quite know what the position is. I suppose we can find out somehow." Paul barely heard her. He was too occupied in trying to understand this new development. "Funny" he thought, "I feel the same as before, what's changed?" Moira caught the drift of his puzzlement and smiled, took him by the arm and steered him to a bench a few feet away.

"Your friend, Sean, says when you fit, you fit. That's all. And you know he has a knack of saying the right thing." As they sat down, Josephine remained standing, an understanding smile on her face.

"You won't want me around, will you! I'll leave you to

yourselves. Catch up with you later!" And she was gone.

Who's she?" Paul asked, not really interested although she was very attractive. He was too busy trying to come to terms with his apparent up-grading - was it that?

"A very clever, and very developed lady!" Moira replied, "Highly developed, even before she came to this realm. I'll get her to tell her own story later; you'll find it very interesting." She changed the subject.

"Oh, but it's good to see you here! I knew you would open up to the reality that is you, and not all that crap you had around you!" Paul stared at her in amazement. He had never ever, heard her talk like that before, not ever. She laughed.

"Yes, I said it, but you see I've discovered that some words are much more suitable than others at times. I didn't say that to shock you; I'm just being honest. You get that way here, you know."

"So now, you've got rid of a lot of the overburden we all carry back there, all the stuff encysting thought and habits in a totally materialistic world." Paul sat staring with his mouth open. "Oh, boy, has she changed!" he thought, "She's much more relaxed and easy-going ..." His thoughts continued, so surprised, that he forgot she was getting it all.

She gave a little chuckle, "Yes, that's right," she said, "I have changed – for the better, I hope. You know just how er - proper society is controlled by hidden standards and hypocrisy - you know the old Victorian ideas about behaviour and so on. You know, like my mother, bless her!"

"Well, that's not necessary here, so we say what we think, except if is likely to hurt someone, then it's better left unsaid. As you have no doubt found out, we keep a check on our thoughts, mainly because if we didn't there would be such a racket, everyone shouting and nobody listening or hearing anything."

"But I say 'Damn' if I want to and nobody cares!"

Paul half heard her explanation. He was occupied more in enjoying how she had changed. She had stripped off the layers of conditioning and teachings of so-called civilisation, to adopt an easy air – no he thought, not that, but more natural, more her true self, more relaxed, more loving even.

He realised as well, he had witnessed the same changes in Jane, but from the opposite direction: where Moira had descended from her lofty perch to be a sensitive loving soul, Jane had risen from the degrading life of a whore to a similarly sensitive loving soul.

Of course, it was inevitable that Moira understood him perfectly. She gripped his arm and moved closer. "Yes, dear Paul, I think you're absolutely right, but don't forget to include yourself in this. I seem to have caught a snatch of a picture from Jane when I came to see you in your little village, do you remember?" He nodded, and she continued, "Jane's picture of you then, was that you had opened up to be the real Paul. She saw it then, and of course, I've seen it too, now."

Paul sat, slightly embarrassed, wondering if he had gone all soft. Hell, he had always been out for Number One, looking for the main chance. Hell, could he have changed that much? He had grown, 'Grown up?' He groaned inwardly, wondering, "Was there a difference?" Was it more grown up, more manly, to be cynical, hard – without mercy or understanding of one less fortunate, or should he help him without hesitation or judgement? From his very depths, he now knew – not fully consciously as yet- that to see another less fortunate than himself, raised the thought, "There but for the Grace of God, go I" and be no less of a man,

Moira knew he would soon be more comfortable as he came more to terms with his true self. She knew he was trying to back off accepting such ideas; it would be better to leave it for now. A change of subject was needed.

"You haven't told me of your doings and things since you went tearing off from the cottage we first went to. I'd love to hear it – all of it!"

Paul gave a little snort. "What, all of it?"

An Old Friend

They sat, arm in arm, gazing out over the lovely, tranquil scene. Boney, now exhausted, stretched out beside Paul. He fondled his ears as he looked down at the resting dog. Thinking anew how animals could share this realm with them. A voice from behind said softly,

"You see my young friend, all red-blooded creatures, share the same etheric substance as ourselves." Paul turned to see a tall man standing behind him, who asked smilingly, "May I sit? I have been watching you and your beautiful friend, including that beautiful creature beside you."

"Yes, of course," Paul answered, "How do you know who we are?" He really knew the answer to this but felt he had to ask.

"My very good friend, Father Sean, told me about you. And, I was quite impressed, as it appears we have already met albeit many years ago. Some centuries, in fact. I was impressed then as I am now. We – Sean and I and a few others like us, reached the opinion that you – both of you, are ready to reach out. To broaden your base, so to speak. Sean insisted that I be the one, as I was a teacher once, and I have other experiences I am sure you will find of great interest..." he paused diffidently, "if you would like to expand your horizons."

A little saying Sean had used came to Paul's mind, "Any knowledge one gains, immediately raises more questions than it answers."

With a little shrug he looked at Moira, questioningly. She nodded, "We can only gain from it." She turned to the man, "What have you got for us then?"

"First, let me introduce myself. My name is James Pillinger, although I expect that means little to you, Paul may have a little jog of memory." He looked at Paul, eyebrows raised in question. Paul shook his head. "Later maybe…"

"At the beginning of the 20th century, I along with a party of scientists, went on an expedition to the Far East, visiting India, Tibet, China, Nepal, Gobi Desert, and Persia to name a few. We spent three years going to many places that seemed outwardly very primitive, all were remote, and my friends, I mean remote!"

"We were met by a group of men who were to be our guides, and it turned out, much, much more than that. Our first surprise was immediately on arrival. Our head guide welcomed us all by name, and speciality, and obviously knew things about us that only we, ourselves would have known or so we thought. All of which he reeled forth, cheerfully, and with the greatest respect. Then he took us to our quarters, where we found to our surprise again, that although we were many miles from the nearest electricity, the place was warm, cosy and well lit, it being quite late in the year."

"This leading man, I'll call him, not his real name of course, was someone very special. For we later found out birds flocked to him, settled on him, flowers nodded their heads as he walked past, and animals would approach without fear. He could fondle a tiger in safety. That was by no means the total of his gifts."

"We immediately thought of him as a very clever trickster, but several other things he would often do, soon tore that idea to shreds."

"Now, you know there are many things can be done here, but not on the Earth-plane. Paul, has done these things, moved about where ever you wanted to go" Paul nodded. "Well, this man would actually appear in my room as I was working. He might chat a while, then go as he came. I got quite used to his comings and goings! This, we knew, was impossible, even the Great Houdini had limits. Not our friend. He was constantly telling us that what he was doing was natural – not magic or any other trick. Over the entire three years we were confronted by many instances of a like nature. In fact, he set up a demonstration for– something that we could prove ourselves."

"We were to go to another village, four days travel away. He suggested he stay behind in this place, with one of our party – yet they would be at our destination when got there. Well, we had to see!"

"It was all set up and away we went. We arrived duly at the new site toward evening, and he appeared as we entered the cottage set aside for us. He asked us to check the time, which was 4.30pm, he chatted awhile then disappeared again. Four days later the man we had left behind as a witness turned up. He said he had stayed at the first village for four days and then at 4.30 said "I'll go now" and disappeared. He then appeared to us in the new village."

"We were flabbergasted, of course. We now had cast iron proof of something we could not understand. Many more things like that happened. We were fed from empty bowls, suddenly being full of tasty, good food. Bread being broken into many pieces but still the same size as at the start, walking on water, through fire and even through solid walls."

"All these things, they insisted were completely natural things. We met many people who were hundreds of years old, looking as you both look now. We met people who you would think would be anything but friends, walking arm in arm, laughing and talking in the friendliest, in fact loving tones."

"Many times, we were blessed, as that is the only word for it, by the presence of the greatest master known to man the "Master Jesus" As he spoke, he rose and stood. Deep respect and awe lighting his face."

"Master, Master" Before them a blindingly bright light slowly formed into a figure. A tall, graceful figure, a little smile on his face. He floated towards them, settling slowly down on the ground. He said nothing but his words were crystal clear, "Dear Friends, may I sit with you a little while? I love talking to new friends." Without further ado his legs folded beneath him as he settled down to their height, as the thoughts came again.

"My young friends, I am just another man, do not hold me in awe. I'm not the same as yourselves, as my friend James here can confirm" But Paul blurted out "But…but…you…"

"People call me Master, but I am just as you! I have lived many years, but this is the same body I had back in Judea. I am able to live here in this realm, or sometimes on the Earth-plane, as our friend James can tell you. He is one of our messengers, like your friend Sean, both very dear trusted friends of mine."

"The point of all our teachings are focussed on individual consciousness, and the way to increase one's understanding. That is indeed your first step, as I'm sure that is your intention to further yourselves, you may think you are so far behind, and below many others, such as your new companion, but let me assure you that while I tell you that I am as you, I mean that I am the son of our beloved Father: I did not say I am the son of God; I said we, note 'we' - are of our Divine Father'. I have been misquoted many times on that subject! But, my dear young friends, you must also know that I said many times to all who would listen to me so long ago, that as I am, so you can be, and what I do, you can do. Along with some other things, this seems to have been lost over the years."

"James, here, has witnessed many things to bring himself – and others - to the understanding of the unending love and wisdom of our divine father. I urge you to listen to him. I am glad to talk to you, my young friends. My love goes to you both. I shall watch with interest your learning." As he spoke, he became less visible, and along with his silent words, he silently faded away and was gone.

Paul clutched Moira's hands in a vice grip, staring at the place where the Master had sat before them. At long last, he remembered to breathe and gulped air, trying to realise who it was; who visited them? In confusion, he turned to James, who calmly nodded and answered,

"Yes, it was, you know! That was Jesus of Nazareth, in person! He came to us many times during our visit to the Far Eastern areas, and he taught us many things, such that I hope to pass on to you, if you wish it. I offer you the progress to the higher levels, if you have a mind to, that is. It must be your choice."

He looked at them in turn, one to the other, waiting for the response he felt sure he would get.

"Yes, but… but what about all this religious stuff? Sean seemed to scorn most of it, even when he was a priest. At that moment Sean, himself, sauntered up to them, grinning smugly as he sat down on the grass. Paul turned to him. "Why didn't you tell me?" he demanded. "James here tries to tell us it was Jesus who sat here with us just now! That's not true, is it?"

Sean nodded, still smiling. "Have you ever known me to mislead you. Or lie to you?" He raised his eyebrows, still grinning.

"No, but ..." "No 'No, Buts.' at all You ought to know all kinds of surprises await you here, and even myself or James here are not immune from that! Yes, my dear Paul, that was indeed who just called, as casually as a neighbour, which his is, of course!"

Paul looked at him, surprise, disbelief, some shock and bemusement, crossing his face. "But… But does this man mean that there's really a man called Jesus Christ? He didn't look like Christ to me. His appearance…all shining like that…why was that? And aren't we supposed to worship him?"

"That's what most people think! But did he look like someone who wanted to be worshipped? No I don't think so, do you? No. As for the religious thing, you will find that out if you study religion, any of them, you will find that they all contain many things which have developed down through the years which were never part of the original teachings of the masters. In fact, a little study will show that the basics of the three main religions are almost verbatim with each other." he gave a rueful little laugh.

"We had an experience when Gautama Buddha, and our just departed visitor acknowledged just as they embraced in full recognition of each other, and their shared love. We were also given to understand that Mohammed was included in that brotherhood. No, Paul we do not follow creeds and dogma of any religious group, either here or on Earth. We are here at the source of all life, all love, all wisdom, and all power."

James continued, "This places us at the forefront, the cutting edge, as you might say, of the enormous potential open to those with the courage to take a step out into the unknown to take to take up the heritage awaiting us."

"No, my dear Paul! Religion holds mankind to a restricted pattern. A stultifying life, dictated by some men who pretended to know all about Heaven, Hell, God, and Satan. Unfortunately, they may as well tell fairy stories, about bogey men to swallow you up on a dark night! Anything to terrify you enough into coming along to church and fill the plate with your hard-earned money! Our friend Jesus knows all about that: how he was completely misunderstood by even his own followers, how now, two thousand years later, he is just able to get his real message across to us, beleaguered misled humanity."

"When I look at what the early Christian church did to expand and rule for a thousand years, the incredible violence of those times, just to achieve and retain power and prestige! No, my young friends, our loving friend Jesus has a much kinder path, inspired of an eternal loving Father, brings me to jump with sheer joy for the awakening I received in the far East."

As James stopped speaking, Paul looked from Sean to Moira, to James, back to Sean, looking for a direction, a lead for his overloaded mind. He reached out again to Moira, almost pleading for something to say. James cleared his throat and reached out to touch Paul's shoulder. "If it helps, he spoke softly, almost apologetically, "I had no idea Jesus would come to us like that! I must have been thinking of him."

"Yes…but" Paul took a deep breath, "But him coming like that means Religion, doesn't it? I never have believed that stuff, and it would take some convincing to believe it now."

"Paul," Sean spoke up "Paul, will you believe me! This is not religion! This is the whole thrust of what we are now trying to do!

Don't you see, the truth as given by such masters as Jesus leaves the churches floundering around in a sea of darkness, their numbers dwindling, their churches closing as the people lose faith in them! No, my dear boy, we'll have to get Jesus to tell you much more about our future! Trust us, Paul! I promise you will not be sorry!"

"It'll be alright, Paul" Moira took his arm, "I'm sure everything will be..." "Sean" he turned to his friend. "You have never let me down, yet, but I'm so damned confused. Just when I think I am starting to get some little understanding of what the hell this place is all about, something comes along to shake what I'm coming to grips with..." he ended abruptly as he stared at a spot just ahead, and as the others followed his gaze, they saw once again the forming of the very bright area a few feet away.

It was the Master again, and he came forward and laid his hand on Paul's shoulder. Immediately a feeling he could only describe as a thrill swept through him. He staggered slightly as the pulse of pure energy coursed down his back and left an impression of peace with what he could only think of as a wonderful vista of an indescribable future with many events intermingling, many people far beyond his perceived status.

He stood transfixed by the impact, the figure he had to accept as Jesus, spoke in a gentle, friendly tone. "I understand your reluctance to become involved in religious things, my young friend! I wonder, would you like me to sit awhile, and I perhaps, can ease your mind, and also show you how you and your lovely lady can help each other. As well as any others you may influence."

They both reached out as one in total trust, to the man before them. They both spoke, "Could we?" "Could you?" In almost total unison, they held out their arms in entreaty. The master nodded with his little smile. "That is why I have returned to help you. I see you were disturbed when I so suddenly came to you. Please, forgive me! I should not forget how different my ways must seem to you, as you come from a world very removed from my normal habitat. But I must introduce you to more uplifting things, for that is indeed the world I so dearly wish to bring to my brothers and sisters. This is the world I tried hard to bring to my friends back in the hills of Judea."

"So little was understood then. So much also was misunderstood, sadly, after I left as well. But I see you want to ask me something." He looked at Paul. "Yes, Sir…may I call you Sir?" The master nodded with a little grin. "Sir, were you crucified to take away the sins of mankind? That's what we are taught, but I find it hard…"

"Yes Paul, I too find it difficult, because those who were close to me, knew what I taught. It saddens me to know that this belief has become the cornerstone of the religion founded in my name, for it is not true. I had been asked on several occasions if healing someone took away their sins, or misdeeds, and my answer was always that I could not, and there was only one person who could wipe away sin, and that was the person who committed it."

"It is also wrong to believe that God will forgive a sinner. God neither forgives nor condemns. God reaches out his hand, his loving arms and enfolds all, saint or sinner into his embrace. But, my dear Paul, do not confuse God with religion! God has no religion: it is only Mankind who finds he needs religion. So, man does a deed, and that deed returns for him to experience, good or bad. No, I demonstrated one thing only; That there is no death! I allowed the authorities to kill me, they thought, but I did not die. Here I am, the same one they crucified. I am changed, of course, and that is indeed possible for all to achieve, but it may take a while to reach the point where I now exist. That, and that alone, was the point of that exhibition, you might well call it."

"As I think of that, may I introduce you to a very old and loving friend?" He rose to his feet and turned to welcome the figure approaching. He was dressed, Paul recognised as a Roman, of probable high rank. He was right, for Jesus introduced him by name.

"Welcome my dear brother!" He turned to the little group, "This is my beloved friend!" and as they embraced, Paul was dumbfounded to hear, "My dear brother, Pilate!" He turned with a wave, "These are my new young friends from the present-day realm of old Earth, and they would like to hear you speak to them." Pilate stepped forward.

"Greetings, young ones. I have come a very long way from that day in Jerusalem so long ago. I did my duty, I thought, as a Roman, but failed to act as a responsible leader. I suffered many years after that, before my awakening!' He embraced Jesus again, and they both sat down in front of Paul, Moira, James, and Sean.

"Now I can see another question, which has caused many to stumble." The master paused, looking thoughtfully at them. "The vexing question of God, our Divine Father." "When I said 'I am the door' I meant that the 'am' in each door is the door through which the light, power, and substance of the Great I Am, which in God, comes forth as an expression in the individual. This 'I am' has but one mode of expression, and that is through ideas, thoughts, words, and acts. The 'I am' God being which is power, substance, intelligence is given form by consciousness. For this reason, I said 'according to your faith, be it unto you, and all things are possible to them that believe.'"

"The next great truth to be revealed through this consciousness is that each individual is held in God's mind as a perfect idea. We have been perfectly conceived and are always held in the mind of God as perfect beings. By having this realisation, we can contact the divine mind, be one with it, bring it forth into expression. In the stillness, the God-mind in all its splendour, illumines the consciousness. God is one and all things, visible and invisible, are one with him. The mind of God floods the consciousness as sunshine floods a darkened room, permeating everything in the universe and freeing man from every limitation, according to his faith."

"All things are possible when man knows that God mind, power, and substance are already with in him."

"It is the belief that 'separation' from God that has caused our sickness, age, poverty, and death."

The young couple sat, arms twined round each other, staring in awe at the two figures before them. They could do nothing but accept that they were indeed in the presence of two of the most important men in history; Jesus of Nazareth, sitting casually beside the ancient governor of Judea, Pontius Pilate! More unbelievable – they were close friends!

Paul looked to Sean, then to James for some confirmation that he was not either dreaming, drunk or insane. James nodded in reassurance. "Yes, Yes… you are not dreaming; I have had the pleasure of meeting both…"

Jesus gave a little chuckle, "My dear James, do not hesitate to address us as you would speak to your close friends. We are, you know, and while we may be somewhat immortal in your sight, we are quite normal!" He turned to the young couple, "I see you are feeling a little overwhelmed and will need time to absorb what I have just said. But you have a distinct advantage over my very dear brethren of Galilee, wonderful men all, but I choose them for their innocence and purity, not for their sophistication." He grinned again at Paul's perceived surprise at the Masters' words. "Do not forget, dear Paul, I have been everywhere on old Earth and have, by such, old contacts with people from everywhere. Have learned much and have even developed a knowledge of modern physics, just out of interest."

Paul gave a little shake of his head. Since his arrival in this upper realm, he had received many surprises, but this latest capped all of them. Here was the man believed to be divine, the son of God, giving the impression he was just another being, albeit a very advanced one. Does that mean the Bible was a load of....

"No, dear Paul, not junk!" Jesus leaned forward. "There is a thread running through it which is sometimes difficult to see. Also, some of the facts of my time in Judea are mis-quoted, and in some cases missing altogether, mostly because the scholars since those days could not accept some of the things I did. The idea that I was unique in being the Son of God is a big misunderstanding. I tried to convey that all, every person is a son or daughter of God. That is the real truth. As I look at you, I see God, our divine Father, shining forth from your faces. Discuss my words with your friends and you will come to a greater understanding."

Paul realised that Jesus was about to depart but longed to ask one more quick question. Jesus perceived it immediately and replied.

"Where is Heaven and Hell? As far as I have ever been able to discover, Heaven exists only in the minds of Man, and he has no other basis for existence. Hell is of a like nature, it is only in the imagination of Mankind, and has been since time immemorial, to terrify simple minded folk into submitting to the whims and fancies of power-hungry priests. This has been carried on into the present time, but it is fast losing some power to bring fear to simple folk.

"Now you have enough to ponder on, so we will leave you for the present, to give you time to understand what we have said, as it is strange to you. We will come again soon. Your friends will help you." He and Pilate stood up, and with arms around their shoulders, walked away and faded out of sight as they went.

Paul let out the huge breath he had been holding and looked from Sean to James and back several times. "Man, Oh Man!" And was lost for any further words. Moira recovered enough to say, in a trembling voice, "But he was so natural! He was just like anyone else, Wasn't he?" James replied, "Yes, he was always like that when we met him in many places on our travels. What struck most of us was that not only the Master Jesus, but many other masters we met were all very humble men: Never any pretensions of any greatness, and you saw none of that here."

James continued, "I must say that the overlying impression the master brings, I'm sure you recognise, is love, unconditional love. Remember, he is well known for that, if for nothing else."

"Another thing we knew nothing about." Moira spoke up again, this time with better control of her voice, "we get no idea from the Bible that Jesus ever smiled or was happy. Did you see his eyes! They were sparkling with fun, I think. And that lovely smile!"

"Yes," Paul pulled a face, "But these times are a bit different from those days; I mean things got a bit tough sometimes with so many gunning for him… He had to be pretty quick on his feet to stay clear of those priests!" James joined in. "Yes, I understand there were times when he had to use all his ability to stay ahead. It seems there were things left out, as He said just now, the times when he was being very hard-pressed by his enemies. They had him tied up, and meant to do him permanent damage, but he just disappeared from their midst. He did something similar just now! They just faded out!"

They all sat in silence trying to absorb their experience, that they had been so honoured by. Paul finally shook himself and said, almost whispered, "What worries me, is that way he seemed to know just what we, or particularly, me, was thinking about. Are my thoughts no longer private now?" Sean gave a little laugh. "Of course, they are! But remember, the thoughts you had were actual questions, were they not?" Paul nodded. "Therefore, the master understood the question. Now, I suggest you both take a stroll, with that lovely dog," Boney raised his head, fully knowing he was being talked about. "Go and wander, and maybe see your friend Joy!"

They both realised that would be a very good idea, and as they stood up, they discovered they were alone. Their friends had both gone. They slowly wandered off aimlessly, arms linked, and minds locked trying to grasp the importance, the reason even, for being visited by such incredibly exalted beings. What had they done to be so privileged? Two very ordinary young people, living ordinary lives, neither good nor bad, just a very average young couple, cast together because of an accident, now here in a realm the master had said was not heaven. Had they heard correctly? No, he did not say this was not heaven; they realised that what he did say was that heaven was all in the mind. Was that what he said? Paul had a distinct feeling that they had missed something.

"We'll have to put that one on the back burner until we can clarify that," Paul shook his head. The more he thought about it the worse his confusion pressed in on him.

He decided to leave the hard bits out for later and concentrated on the other things he said. And what exactly did he say, he wondered.

So, they strolled. As they sauntered, Boney happily by their side, they were soon absorbed at the variety of different animals around them, many with the humans they had known in their Earth-lives. Moira's two Siamese cats soon joined them, totally without fear of the big black boisterous dog romping around them. Watching him, Paul was drawn to an incident during his boyhood when his uncle had said something that had made a deep impression on him.

This happened during his young, impressionable years, when they were at the river nearby. A young boy of about five years old was playing on the riverbank a little way from them when he slipped and fell into a deep pool. Unable to swim or perhaps panicking, the boy was in trouble. His dog leaped into the water, somehow knowing the boy was in trouble. Paul's uncle ran to the pool, dived in, and was able to pull the child to safety after a tense few moments with the current. The boy was brought ashore and, luckily, was little the worse for his fright. It was some time before they had pacified the child's mother, who had allowed her attention to slip for a moment. She had learnt a valuable lesson. It was then that they discovered that the boy's dog was missing. He was later found - pinned under the branch of a sunken tree, drowned. They tried to hide this from the boy, but he was inconsolable.

Paul's uncle was very quiet on the way home. Paul was supportive. "But you saved the boy, Uncle! I was very sad when Boney died, but he was only a dog!" "Paul! Paul!" his uncle said softly, "Of course you wouldn't know! All animals with red blood have souls, just like us, and very likely, that dog is now in the equivalent of Dog's heaven." Paul had thought nothing of that at the time. In the years between he had completely forgotten about it. As he looked about in this lovely place, he realised just how much he had brushed aside during his early years. And while his family had by no means been religious, they had firm values of the fitness of things, and much had rubbed off on him, although he tried to ignore most of it; it was much too difficult to follow, let alone practice. Now, he had been face to face with the most important man who had formulated much of the western world's thinking, although he was starting to discover how much of it was off course.

Now, looking around the park, he saw just what his uncle had meant so long ago. All these cats, dogs, horses, donkeys - on and on went the list - all these animals had been the loved companions of humans, and the love they had shown was now evident in their presence here. Those two beautiful cats draped around Moira's neck were perfect examples they serenely looked about completely at home there. But, he wondered, what about all the really wild ones? Did they come here too? His answer came almost at once.

"Ho, you two!" they saw a figure approaching - Joy, of course - complete with her beautiful lioness. She said as she got closer, "You didn't get very far with your walk!" "No" Paul shrugged, "We have just been held up, you might say..." "Oh? Who?" Moira could scarcely contain herself. "You'll never guess!" She was just beginning to emerge from the shock they had received.

"Well? Tell me! What happened?" Paul tried to look casual as if it was of no importance, but he could not hide his inner thoughts. Joy pretended anger, "Tell me, you clown, or I'll set Elsa on you!" He took a deep breath and tried to calm down, but there was this burning need to shout it out. He grabbed Joy by the arm and said, almost in a fierce whisper, "We've just met Jesus! Jesus of Nazareth! What do you say to that!" Joy started to laugh. Paul glared, "It's no laughing matter! I tell you we..." Yes, I know!" Joy grinned broadly, "Of course you did! The wonderful man comes here quite a lot, and when he does, all the animals, crowd around him, pushing and shoving, trying to get his attention! He was here a little while ago, in fact, and he had his friend Pilate with him." "Yes, that's right," Moira replied eagerly, "That must have been just before they came to us." "Very likely," Joy nodded, "but I see there is a mystery somewhere. Can I help?"

"All these," He waved his arm at the scene, "were once pets of us humans, on Earth, that's right?" "Yes, you know it is!" "Yes, I do," He raised his eyebrows, "But what about all those that never have any contact with us? Where do they go? What happens to them?"

"Good question!" Joy nodded, "What I understand about it is that all those creatures, without the experience that inevitably raises them up the spiritual or knowingness scale, remain on their own level, belonging to what seems best described as a group soul which comes from what we understand as the Aqueous Substance, from which all things originate. Even us. As you are aware, all the creatures on Earth have a unique place in the order of things, of Creation, and they are necessary to maintain a balance between them."

"The original state was quite different to what is now on Earth. I suppose you were raised with the idea that Man had dominion over all other species, but that did not mean exploitation of them. But not to go too deeply into it, the beginning was..." She hesitated, and Moira spoke up, "Oh, yes, I remember! We talked about that a little while ago, and it seems that all life, including even mankind, were supplied with all their needs from what you said just now, from the aqueous substance - is that right?" Joy nodded, "Right! But while animals do not have the freedom of choice we have, there is a little, for the stronger ones started bullying, the weaker ones, you might say, and we - mankind - soon followed, so today we kill for food, where once we had no need, no need at all! And, of course, we have forgotten that and have no idea what it could be. Therefore, my two young folks, because you are bright enough to look for answers, you are given every chance to grow."

"So, when the Great Master comes again, reach out for all you're worth! Take all he gives and then some! "Now, relax here a while, and dream up a few questions, and you will find that the topics raised will be just what you desire! He will know!" She turned to a donkey trying to get his neck scratched, "Oh, you again?" I'm always fondling you!"

Both Paul and Moira looked at each other, both with the same thought; they were both on the brink of the unknown once more. "Situation normal," he thought. Ever since we came here, we've been almost constantly met by surprises, one after the other. So, what was next? There had to be more. He had found that a lot of religion was good value as far as it went, but why, oh why, did they use it to threaten and frighten people? That is why he had turned away from it. Now, here was the master, casually sitting before them, light-years removed from the usual concept of Jesus Christ. Ah! That was a question needing an answer.

They wandered a while, both aware of their similar thinking. In such beautiful surroundings, the peace and tranquillity were having almost a soporific effect, but there was an underlying niggle. This was a bit foreign; he had been rather casual about such esoteric things as religion, but he had to admit that, on recent experience, there was much more than he knew of.

Now, the appearance of Jesus, not to mention Pilate - and together – sparked off another niggling thought. He needed to know a little more. And at the idea, both Sean and James stood before them.

"Told you, didn't I?" Sean laughed.

"You were right," James agreed with a little snort, "But you've known them now for a while...." "And here's the master now!" And there he was, almost gliding up to them, this time, without his dazzling aura. He explained as he came up to them.

"I'm very glad to see you, my dear friends, but I did not want to be brighter than our Father, whose light you see all around us." He sat before them. "Let us just sit and be loving friends together!" He extended his arms to include them all. "Now, what shall we discuss?" Paul was quick to respond. "Master, could you tell us about the devil and where is hell?"

Jesus quickly replied. "Hell, or the devil, has no abiding place except in Man's mortal thoughts. With your present enlightenment, can you place either in any geographical position on Earth? If Heaven is all and surrounds all, where could he be placed in God's perfect plan? It was only the personal adversary that I cast out. I never saw the devil in any man, save he thought him there himself."

They all sat a few moments soaking it up, then Moira asked, "I would like to know who or what God really is." Jesus answered, "God is the principle behind everything that exists today. Spirit is omnipotent, omnipresent, and omniscient. God is the one mind that is both the direct and the directing cause of all that you see around us.

God is the source of all true love that binds all forms together. God is the impersonal principle. To the individual, he can be personal, all-loving, all-giving father or mother. God sits not on a throne judging people after they die, for God is life, which never dies."

"You can see and talk with God at any time; indeed, he is far closer than any mortal can be, dearer and truer than any friend. God is closer than breathing, nearer than hands and feet. The God that judges, destroys, or withholds good is but a God conjured up by man's ignorant thinking. Then you need not fear that God, unless you wish to do so."

"When I said I am the Christ, the only begotten of God, I did not declare this for myself alone, for had I done this, I could not have become the Christ. I say that in order to bring forth the Christ, or God, in Man. I, as well as all others, must declare it, then must live the life, and the Christ, or God-Man, must appear. When I stepped upon the water, do you think I cast my eyes downward into the depths of material existence? No, I fastened my eyes on God's power that transcends any other. The water became as firm as rock, and I could walk upon it in safety."

Both Paul and Moira were speechless, overwhelmed by the words of the Master Jesus! Moira sat, spellbound by the words, the manner, the relaxed, even cultured voice. That he had come to them, not once, but twice, come to such insignificant a pair, were spun into a riot of thoughts, impressions, and stunned into silence, they both sat, wondering if it was indeed really happening. Sean was the first to break the almost reverent hush, although the master had been to some pains to dispel any pretensions for himself. "Can I bring forth the Christ?" Was the question.

Jesus replied at once, "Yes! Man came forth from God, and he must return to God. The history of the Christ does not begin with my birth nor end with the crucifixion. The Christ was when God created the first man in his own image, his likeness. The Christ and all men, and that man, are one. That the Christ means more than that man Jesus goes without contradiction. For more than fifty years after that day on the cross, I taught and lived with my friends in a quiet place outside Judea. Seeing that they were depending on me rather than themselves, I withdrew in order to make them more reliant. You must see that you are truly divine, and being divine, you must see that all men are as you. As you rise, you lift the whole world with you. The path becomes plainer for your fellowmen. You must have faith in yourself, knowing that that faith is God within. You are a temple of God; you are in God; God is in you!"

For a long time after that, Paul wandered around with Moira, almost spellbound by the Man from Galilee. They had no other thoughts but the simple presence he displayed, no way dominating in manner. There was, however, a quiet authority in his voice. And what he had said had shaken Paul to his very core. He had, in a few words, blown the lid off all the conventions and false beliefs of millions of people the world over. Further, they instinctively knew that all he said fitted Muslims, Jews, Hindus, and all the others.

They realised that in those few moments, they had taken a gigantic leap forward, and Paul gave a wry grin, for they were now on the brink of a golden vista lying ahead, and he could not escape from the quotation that appeared in his head about the man who asked for a light as he went up to the man who stood at the gate. For there was the light before them. They looked into each other's eyes and saw the reflections of their hopes and dreams. Hand in hand, they stepped forth into the light.

They had found their Heaven.